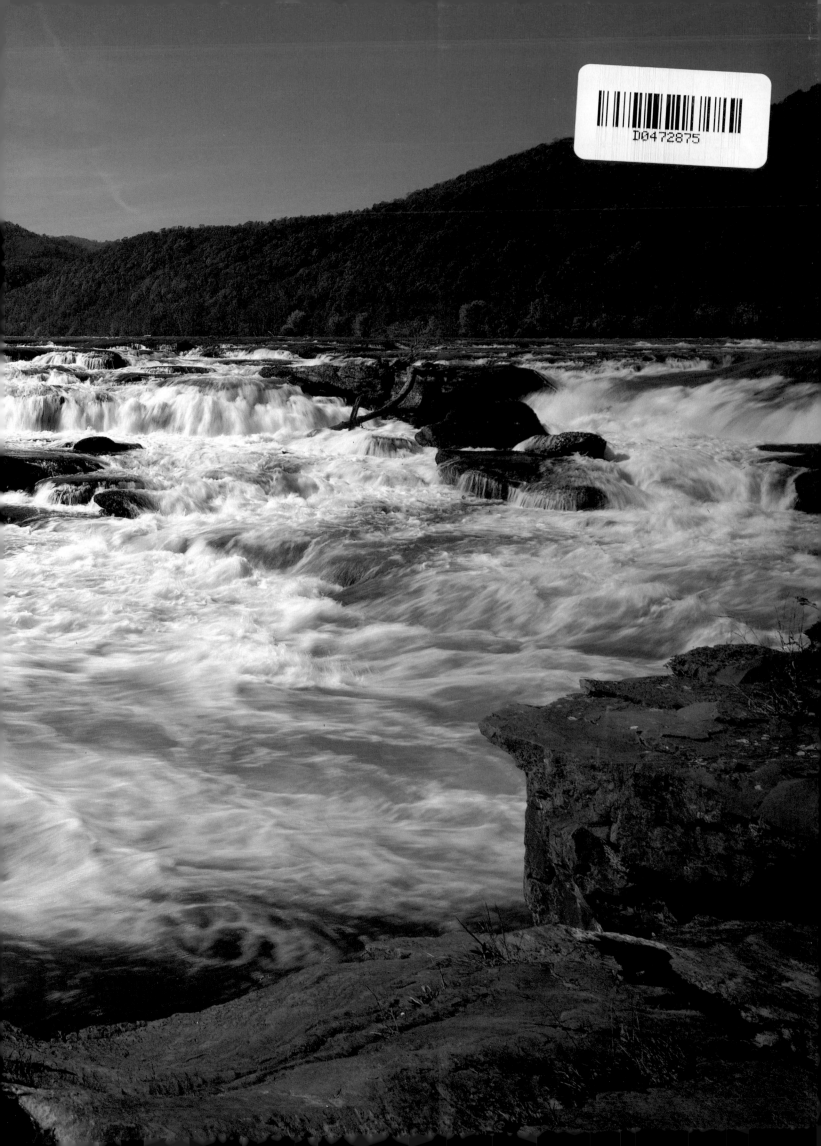

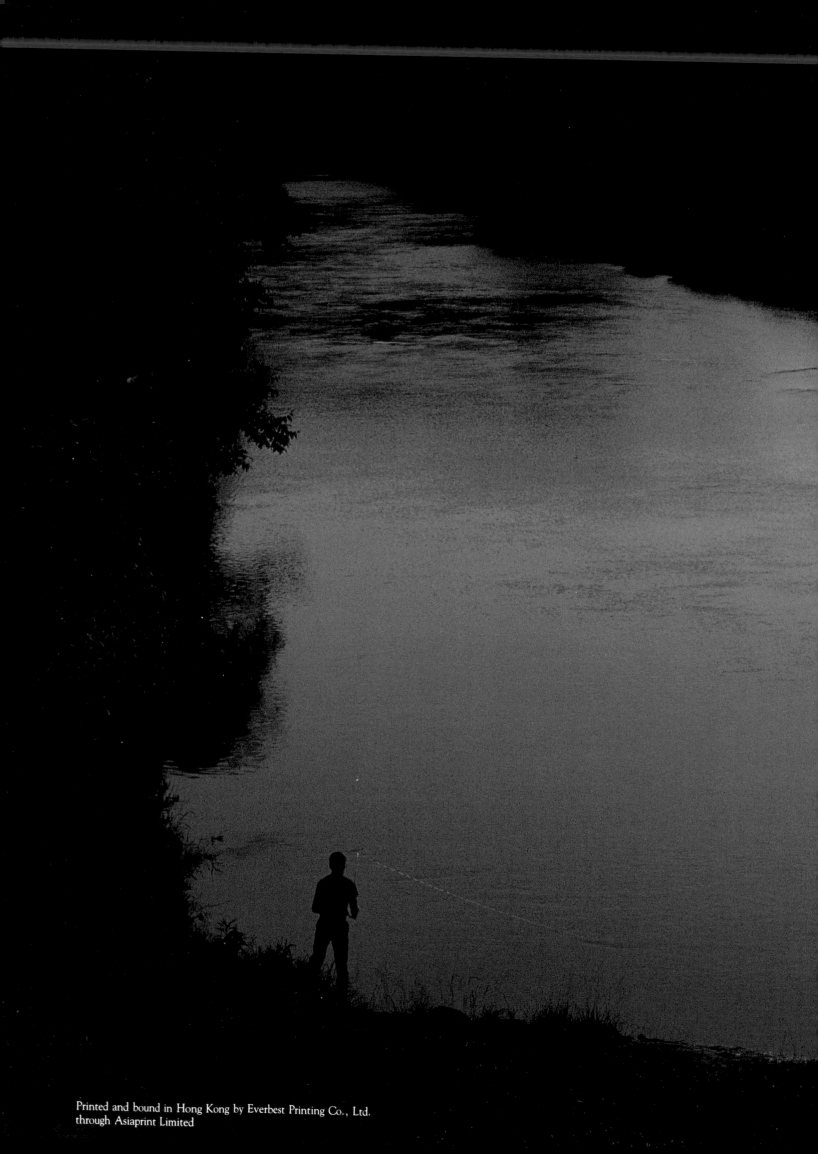

Printed and bound in Hong Kong by Everbest Printing Co., Ltd.
through Asiaprint Limited

Published by:

Cannon Graphics, Inc.

ISBN 0-9623153-1-1

Library of Congress Catalog
Card Number 90-085737

This book may be ordered from:

Cannon Graphics, Inc.
418 Lehigh Terrace
Charleston, WV 25302
304-346-7602

$13.95 plus $2.00 shipping

ACKNOWLEDGEMENTS

First I would like to thank my wonderful family for their support and help on this book. My lovely wife, Teresa, and wonderful daughter, Lucia Katherine. My loving parents who are always there for counsel and help. At the start of this book we approached the rafting companies on the New River for help in obtaining photos of the river. They all offered assistance, so much so that we could use only part of the help offered. For this reason, instead of singling out individual companies we would like to thank this great industry as a whole. We are indebted to the many people who helped in numerous ways such as correcting copy, modeling for photographs, pilots who flew for the aerial photographs, river guides, individuals who made arrangements etc.; Martha Mahlie, Idair Smookler, Chris Taylor, Dewey Yates, Don Kodak, Clarice Weaver, Mr. and Mrs. Lester Hart, Minnie Powell, Kelly Underwood, R. Edward Pinney, Rick Rogers, Scott Miller, Michael Ivey, Cheri Clark, Wanda Chalmers, Greg Allen, Ray Hepner, Randy Johnson, Margaret Bray, John Hartman, Teka K. Lamade. Larry and Gay Cabell, John Hull, Misty Hull, Liz Watts, Joyce Cooper, Chris Dragan, Clif Bobinski, Paul Brewer, Rick Mix, David Strenz, Bob Whitt and Amy Renee Shaluta.

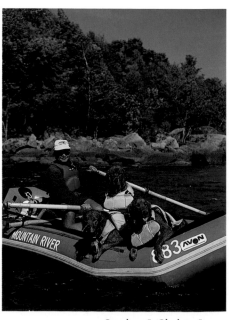

Cover; *Clif Bobinski rafts the lower New with his three golden retrievers. He is the River Operation Manager of Mountain River Tours. His companions are Shaman, a five-year-old male, Supaya Red Feather, a three-year-old female, and Sequoyah Red Feather, a seven-month-old female. Clif says Shaman is an old pro who has rafted the New, Upper Gauley and the Cheat Rivers. In fact, he likes to jump out of the raft and swim through the big rapids. This was Sequoyah Red Feather's first raft trip.*

Dave Cline operated the photo raft for these photos.

Gerald S. Ratliff

Back Cover; *View of the New River from Grandview Park.*

Gerald S. Ratliff

Preceding Overleaf; *Sandstone Falls, north of Hinton.*

Preceding Overleaf; Arnout Hyde Jr.

Stephen J. Shaluta Jr.

NEW RIVER

CONTENTS

INTRODUCTION

The New River is actually a very old river, the oldest in North America and second only to the Nile among the rivers of the world. Geologists estimate the New is older even than the mountains around it, holding to its primordial course as the Appalachian ridges rose jagged from the earth and then mellowed over eons to the worn contours familiar to modern observers.

Today it is the premier river of its region, traversing three states as it collects the waters of a broad swath of the Southern Appalachians. The New travels about 250 miles, beginning as separate north and south forks in the high Smokys of northwestern North Carolina. The two branches converge just south of the state line, and the New leaves the Tarheel State as one stream. It takes in many creeks and small rivers as it passes northwestward across Virginia and picks up the Greenbrier River, its most important tributary, soon after crossing into West Virginia. The New receives the waters of the Gauley at Gauley Bridge, and thereafter becomes the Kanawha River.

The world of the New River is a great highland empire. Whether opening wide, fertile valleys, as it does in Virginia and North Carolina, or slashing the deep canyon that carries it finally to its mouth in West Virginia, the New is always surrounded by green mountains. Its people are mountain people, and it is the business of this book to tell the story of those people and their river.

The human story of the New goes back to man's earliest use of the region, thousands of years ago by current scientific reckoning. Archaeological evidence indicates that the earliest people in the watershed were wandering big game hunters, succeeded by a variety of less nomadic woodland tribes. By the time of first European contact, the valley was largely unoccupied but not unclaimed, a bloody buffer between contending Indian groups. These natives, the fierce Shawnee in particular, gave ground reluctantly, making life a brutal hell for white intruders of the mid-1700's. Mary Draper Ingles was among those who suffered most, carried down the New into captivity in the summer of 1755 and struggling back upstream to her Blacksburg home late the following fall.

The river served the Indians as it served their successors, both as a travel route and a barrier to travel. Canoes glided on tamer stretches of the New's middle and upper sections, while paths and portages circumvented troublesome and sometimes deadly falls and rapids. The wildest portion of the river, its final 50-mile plunge to the Gauley, was generally avoided, with Indian trails taking to the plateau to the north and south. U.S. 60, the historic Midland Trail, now follows the best known of these alternate routes.

Early white settlers made similar use of the New. The river and its tributaries are among what were known historically as the "western waters," flowing to the Gulf of Mexico rather than the Atlantic. The valley of the lower New was recognized as an important corridor westward, envisioned at one time as the final link in the James River & Kanawha Canal proposed by George Washington and other early Virginians. That grand scheme proved abortive. Canal boats never traveled the New, although heavy wooden bateaux transported tons of cargo on some stretches of the river.

Overland travelers found that the New River presented a formidable obstacle, running south to north through a region whose major roads ran east and west. Crossing points were few and far between, and they remain so today. Roads did not follow the northerly course of the New, for the most part, with notable exceptions where the river cuts through mountain ranges. The most important of these cuts comes in southwestern Virginia, where U.S. 460 now clings to the river's steep flanks through the Narrows water gap.

Ironically, the portion of the New that had proved most treacherous to early travelers later became the most traveled section of the valley. The Chesapeake & Ohio Railroad made its way from Virginia across to the Greenbrier River soon after the Civil War. The Greenbrier meets the New at Hinton, West Virginia, near where construction of the C&O's tunnel at the Great Bend of the Greenbrier claimed the life of steel-driving John Henry. River and railroad entered the New River Gorge a few miles downstream from Hinton. The completion of the C&O's New River main line in 1873 transformed the narrow canyon into one of America's busiest thoroughfares, spawning decades of coal mining along the walls of the gorge and a rowdy boom town at Thurmond.

The miners of the gorge received a river that had already seen a world of human drama upstream. The watershed was being extensively timbered by the turn of the century, the trains of the C&O hauling timber as well as coal, and other trains—most colorfully the "Virginia Creeper" that labored along the South Branch—doing similar work elsewhere. Local industry had established itself early on: grist mills, sawmills, iron furnaces and other works limited only by the entrepreneurial imagination—even a shot tower for the manufacture of bullets from falling drops of molten lead. Succeeded in the 20th century by the giant munitions plant at Radford, the early 19th-century shot tower still stands on the banks of the river near the Interstate 77 bridge, preserved now as a Virginia state park.

There's less commotion along the New River nowadays, less mining and less timbering, and in some places fewer people. The once bustling gorge has almost no residents—one that I can think of in the long, lonesome miles below Thurmond. The valley has settled back to quieter times and the people who came there— fishermen, hikers, whitewater enthusiasts, and nature lovers of every stripe—are increasingly attracted by the sparkling river itself. The region welcomes visitors with a major new national park in West Virginia and state parks in each of the states.

This book by West Virginia's finest scenic photographers will guide you through the byways of New River country, past and present. You will travel from the North Carolina headwaters to historic Gauley Bridge, site of Civil War struggle and neighbor to a frightful 20th-century industrial tragedy at the Hawks Nest tunnel. You will follow historic boat trips and rush the rapids with modern day rafters. You will wander the ruins of mining towns and sample the lore of miners, railroaders, and other hardworking people who populate the New River story. It adds up to a memorable tour of a great American river valley, the next best thing to being there. —Ken Sullivan

Ken Sullivan, editor of GOLDENSEAL magazine and West Virginia's folklife director, is a co-founder of the annual New River Symposium. He has published articles in the Appalachian Journal, West Virginia History, and Pennsylvania History, among other publications; a National Park Service book on the New River town of Thurmond; and a 1979 Ph.D. dissertation. His earliest memories of New River are of its quieter stretches in his native Southwest Virginia, but he has since become most familiar with the river's famous gorge in West Virginia.

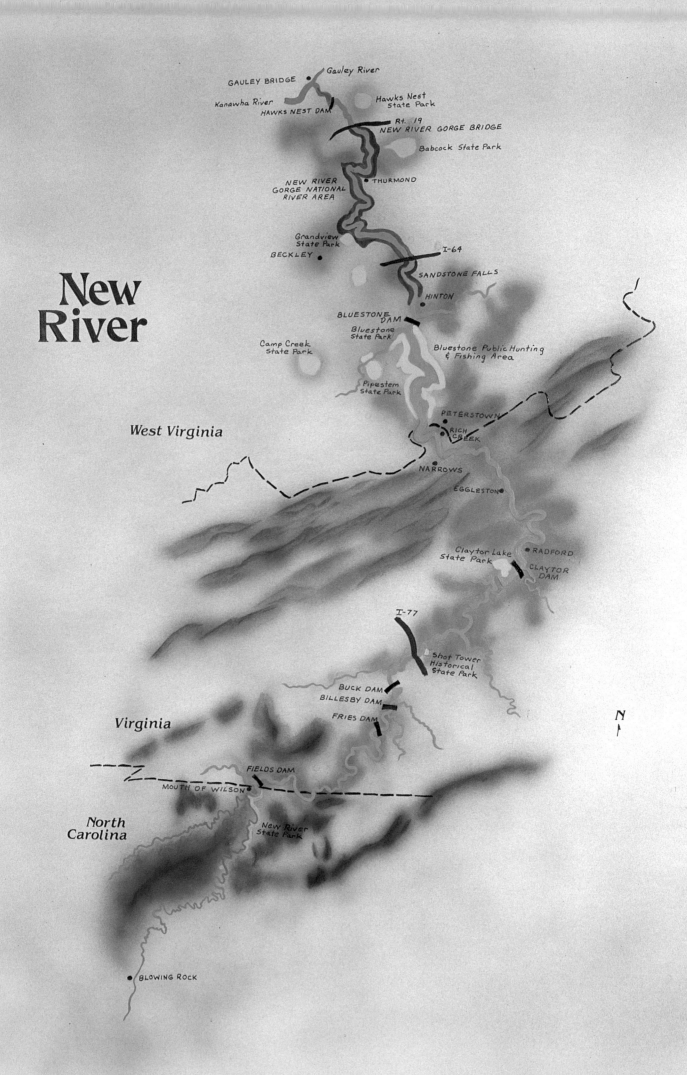

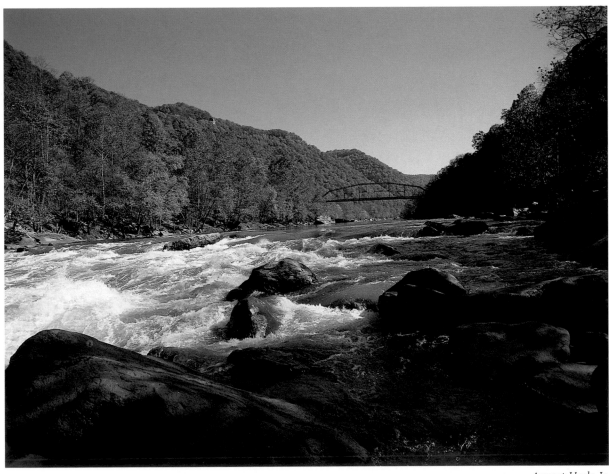

Arnout Hyde Jr.

Fayette Station Bridge, an iron truss bridge built in 1889.

New River map by Rita Damous. She is a graphic artist for the West Virginia Division of Tourism and Parks, with an Associates Degree specializing in Commercial Art from the Art Institute of Pittsburgh.

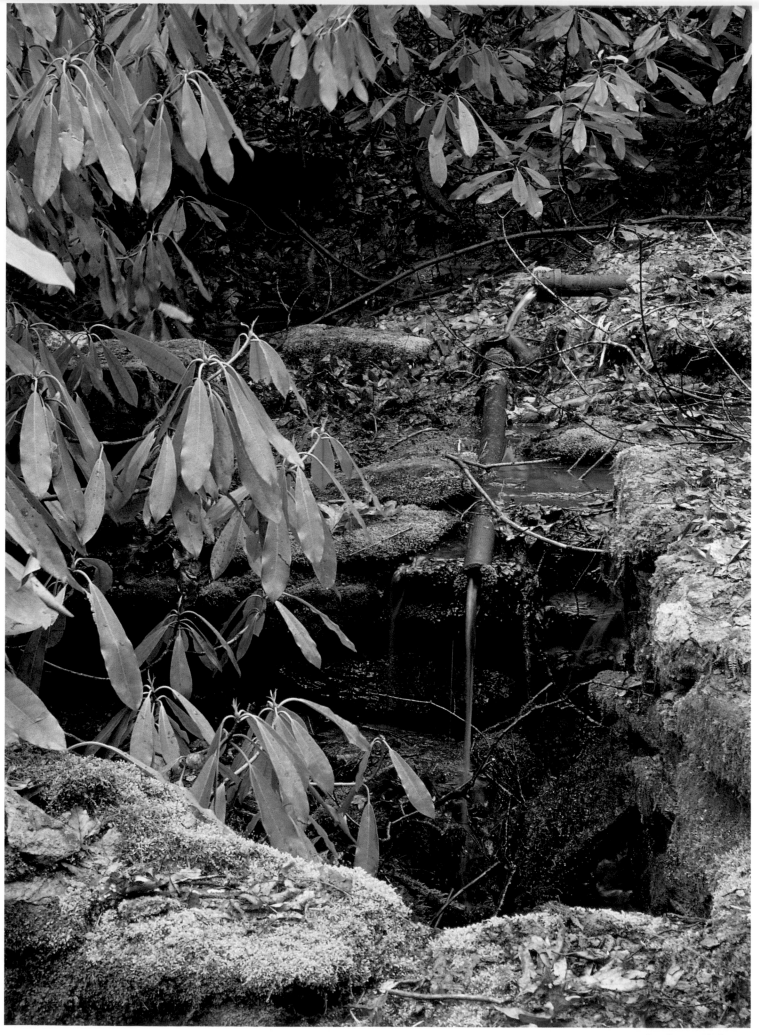

Stephen J. Shaluta Jr.

BIRTHPLACES TO
THE MOUTH
OF WILSON

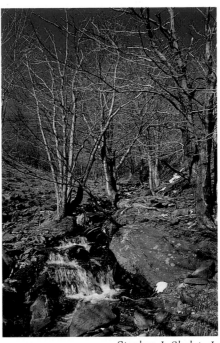

Stephen J. Shaluta Jr.

The North Fork of the New near the headspring on Snake Mountain, north of Pottertown Gap.

A spring at the Blowing Rock Assembly Grounds is one of the birthing places of the South Fork of the New.

High in the Blue Ridge Mountains of North Carolina can be found the sources to the New River. Starting from several springs in the northwestern corner of the state, the South Fork of the New is born. Some miles to the west, small rivulets of water find their way down the slopes and ravines to form the North Fork.

These waterways, ironically, flow in a northerly direction through a mountainous tableland, which, in places, exceeds 4000 feet in elevation. Flowing in this direction, the river has cut through every ridge of the Appalachians, giving credence to the fact that the river was here before the mountains. This land mass is one of the oldest on the North American continent.

As these forks make their sixty-some mile journey to join near the Virginia/ North Carolina border, they pass through rich grasslands and rolling hills. Tarheel farmers grow corn, beans, beef cattle, and evergreen pines for Christmas trees.

Perhaps some 15,000 years ago, the first human species came upon this land: the Paleo-Indian. They left, as archaeological evidence, Clovis Fluted projectile points used to hunt prehistoric big game animals. Later Indian cultures frequented the region leaving burial mounds and artifacts—a record of prehistoric life. In the seventeenth century, the first Europeans visited the area and, some years later, settled the countryside. The river and its valley became rich in rural heritage of early settlements and farms that passed from one generation to another. A few years back, the popular TV show *Andy Griffith*, set in the town of Mayberry, portrayed this wonderful rural countryside.

The river now serves as an important waterway for many recreational experiences such as canoeing, fishing and camping. Today 26.5 miles of the New—federally designated as "Wild and Scenic"—is managed by the North Carolina Division of Parks and Recreation as the New River State Park.

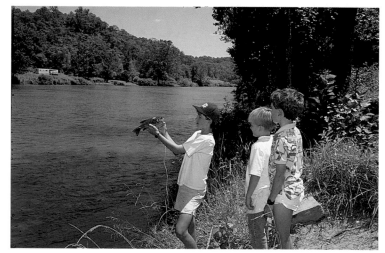

Stephen J. Shaluta Jr.

Right; *A small mouth bass delights children on the South Fork near Piney Creek. Following page; Snake Mountain where the North Fork of the New begins. Bottom; Cattle, which canoers occasionally find difficult to navigate around, find relief on a hot summer day in the South Fork of the New.*

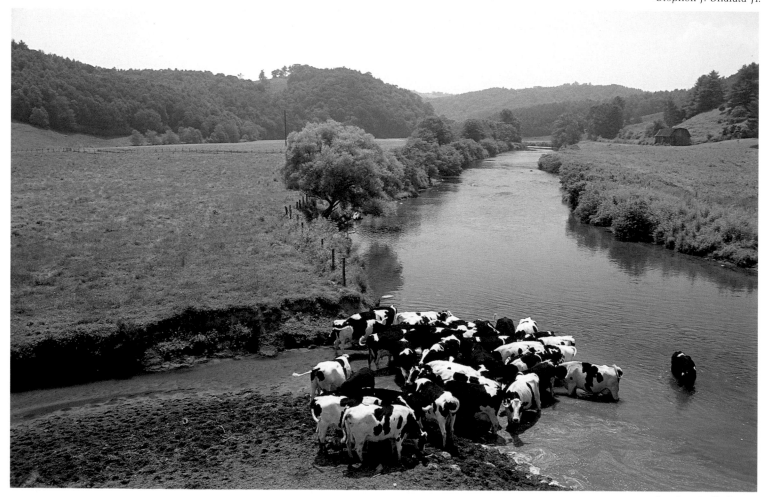

Stephen J. Shaluta Jr.

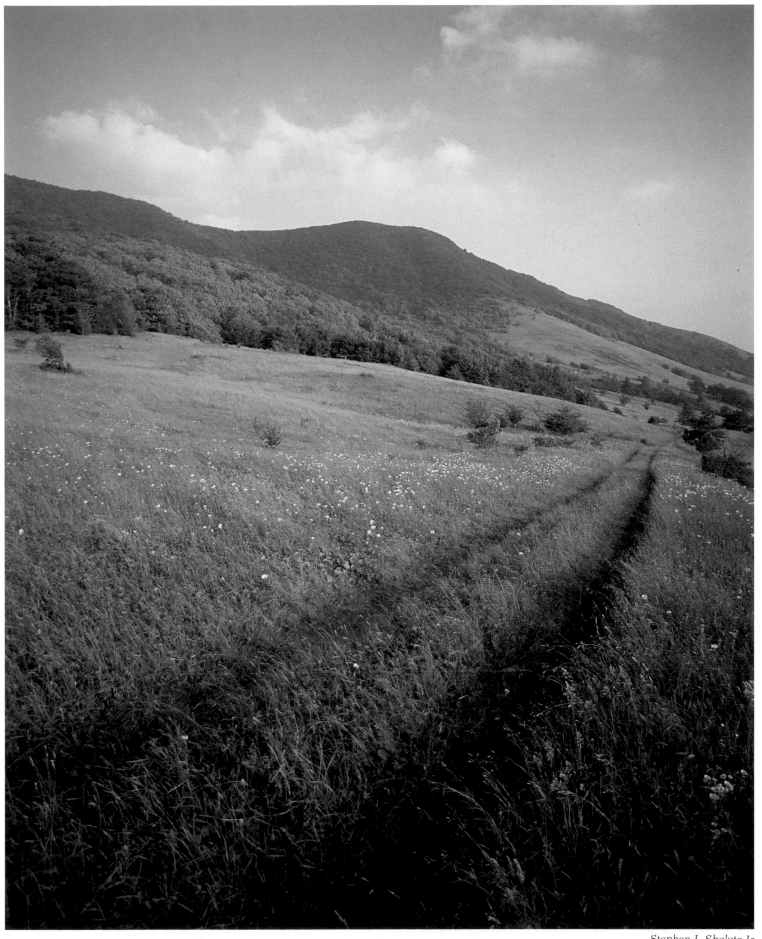

Stephen J. Shaluta Jr.

Overleaf; Looking from Snake Mountain where the drainage area begins for the North Fork of the New.

Overleaf; Stephen J. Shaluta Jr.

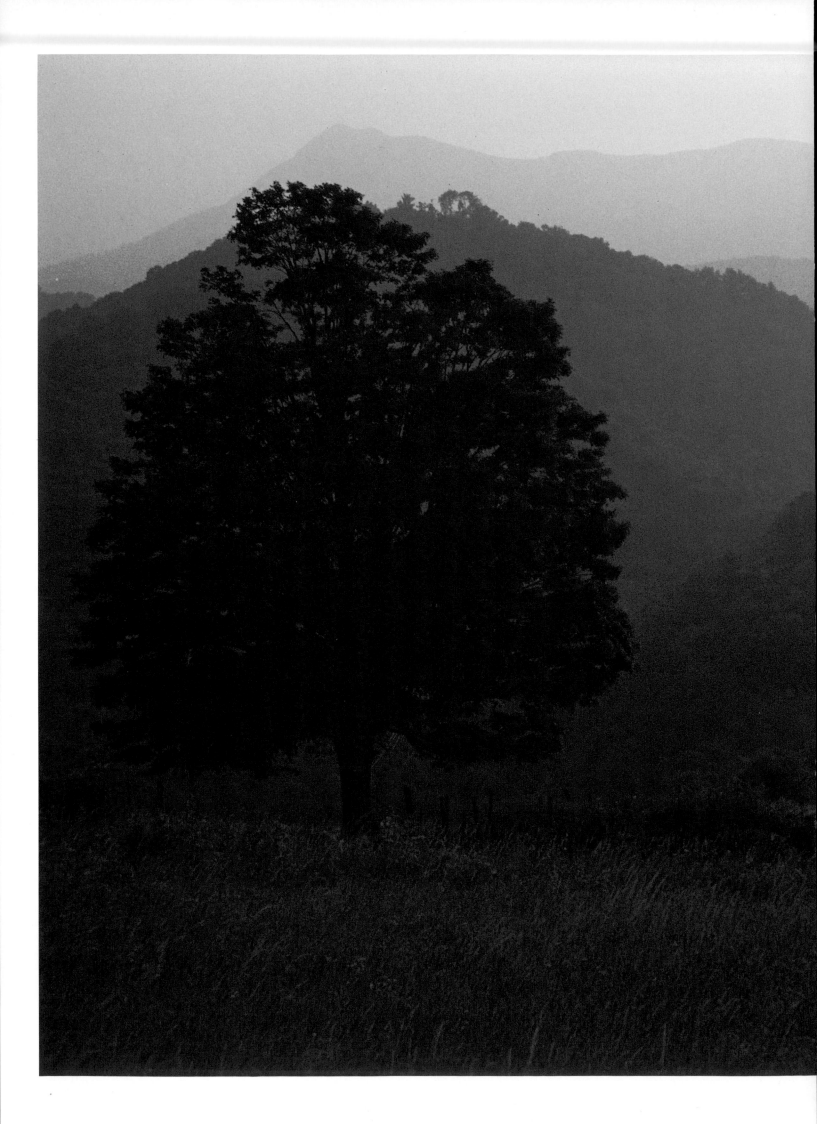

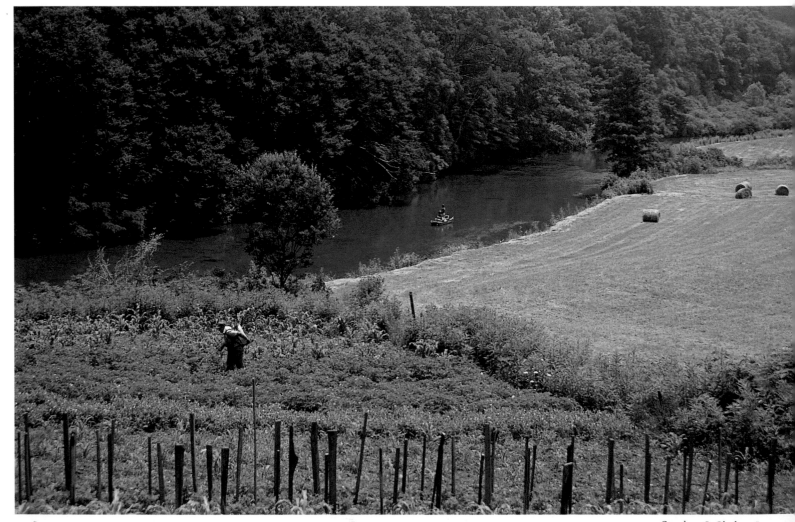

Pastoral scene of the South Fork of the New, upstream from the community of Todd.

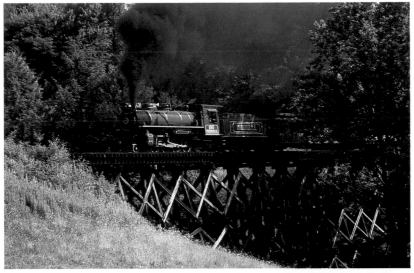

Tweetsie Railroad at Blowing Rock along the South Fork of the New is a popular tourist attraction in the area.

Stephen J. Shaluta Jr.

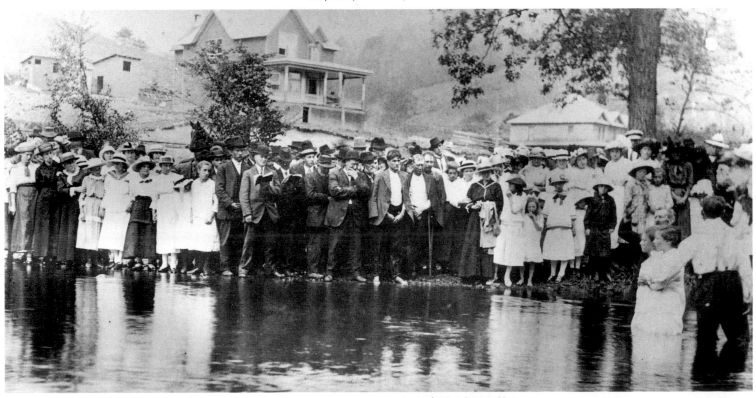

Mr. and Mrs. Lester Hart

Top; An old-time baptizing in the area, Tuckerdale Baptist Church, May 1916. Right; A typical old homestead along the river, a reminder of the past.

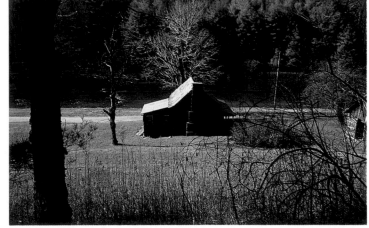

Gerald S. Ratliff

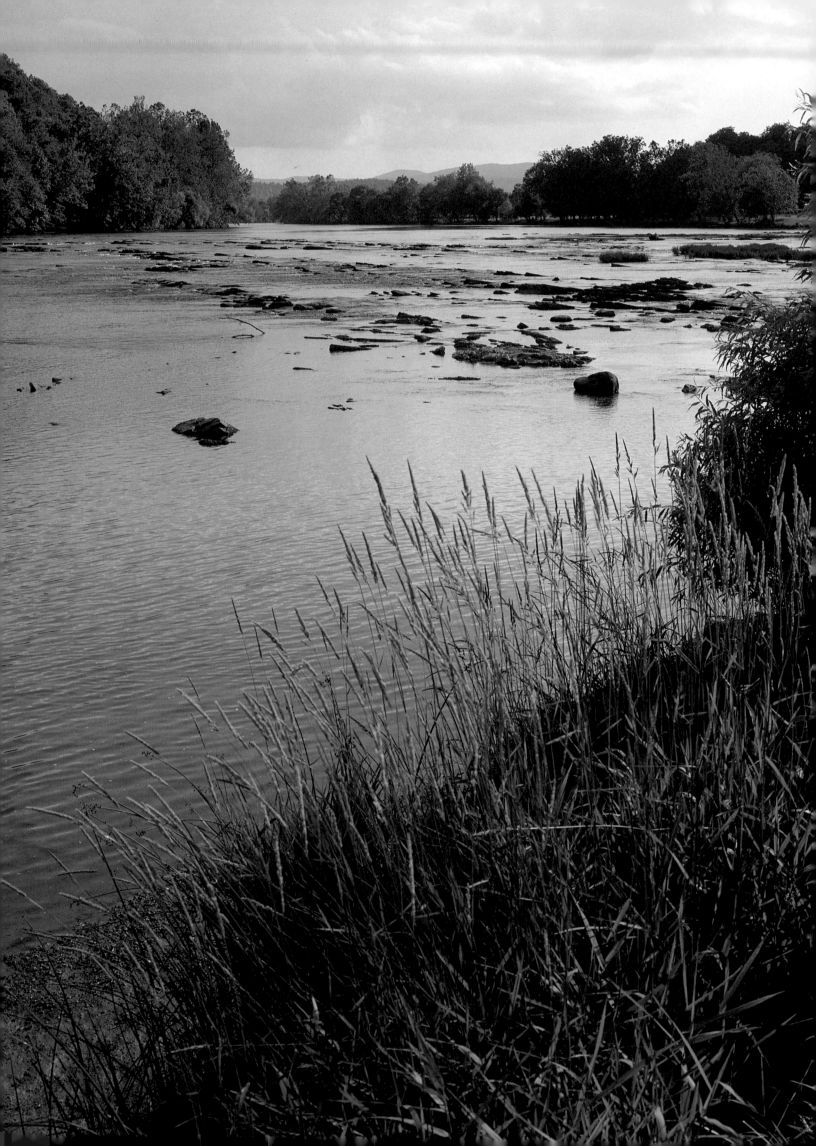

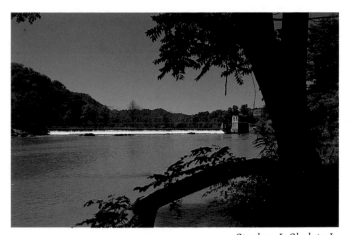

An early dam on the New River near the Mouth of Wilson

MOUTH OF WILSON
TO CLAYTOR LAKE

Evening scene of Shot Tower Rapids.

From the Mouth of Wilson, the New River takes a twisting, turning course through Virginia. In a straight line it is 50 miles from the Mouth of Wilson to Glen Lynn, Virginia; however, by the river route it is almost 150 miles. Throughout its course, broad meadows meet the river on one side, while on the opposite banks there are often steep bluffs.

A series of dams on this stretch of river impedes the flow from its natural course. These dams were built years ago to supply power for textile mills. Typical Virginia river towns grew up around these mills and dams. An 11-foot dam downriver from the Mouth of Wilson supplied power to the Fields Woolen Mill. Still farther downriver, another dam at the town of Fries was constructed in 1900 by a banking magnate named Col. Francis Fries. This 39-foot dam powered a cotton textile mill, which became the lifeblood of Fries. The Byllesby and Bucks dams supply hydroelectricity.

The river supported early extensive lead mining near Austinville. These mines supplied much of the lead for the Confederacy during the Civil War. A shot tower, one of the few such towers left in America, made lead pellets for hunting. In addition to lead mines, remnants of an early iron industry are still visible. A ghost town and remains of an old foundry are on the banks near Foster Falls.

When floating down this stretch of river, a touch of nostalgia is felt while passing the old Virginia river towns, mills, shot towers, old row boats tied to trees, and those excellent old fishing holes.

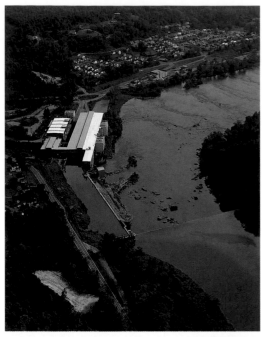

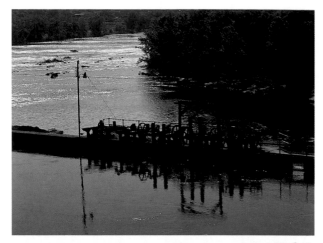

Arnout Hyde Jr.

Arnout Hyde Jr.

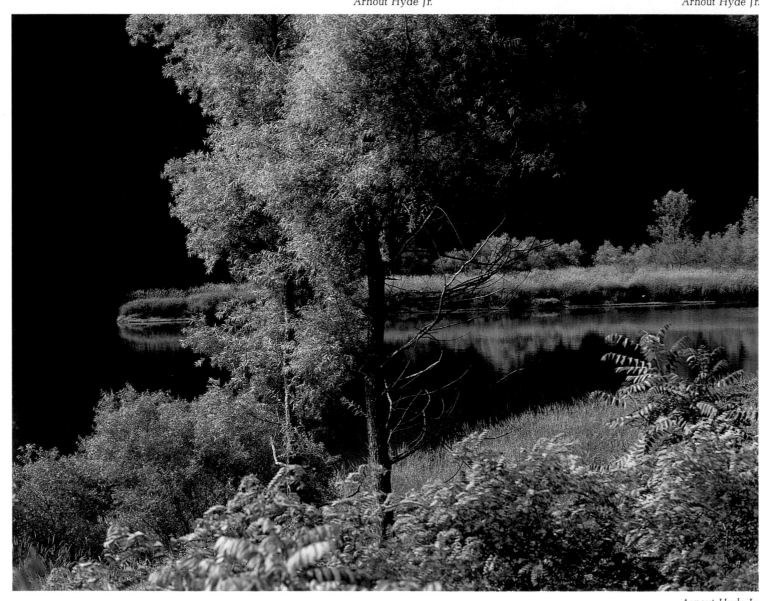

Arnout Hyde Jr.

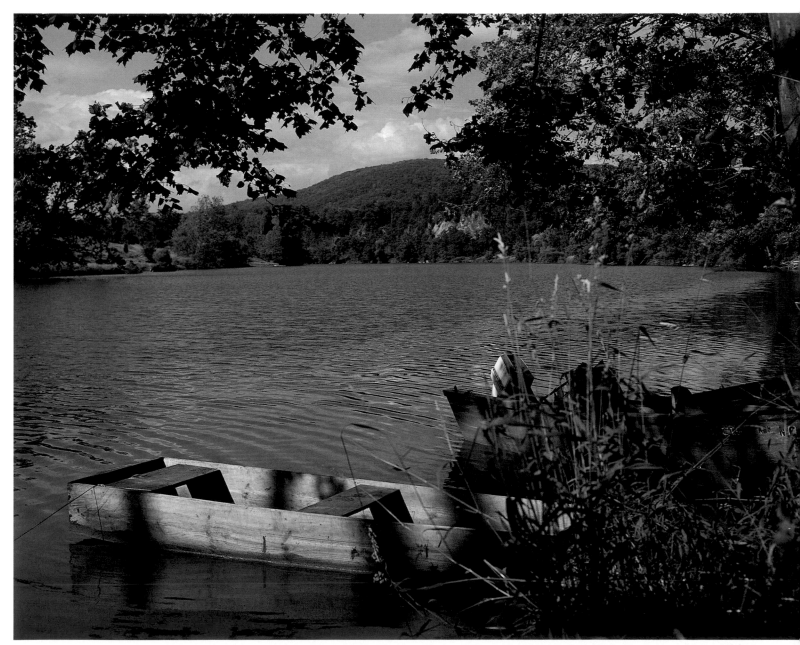

Arnout Hyde Jr.

Top; *Pastoral scene of the river with the Shot Tower Historical State Park on the right bank.* (Opposite Page) Top Left; *Aerial view of the town of Fries.* Top Right; *Valves regulate the flow of the river for the textile mill at Fries.* Bottom; *Still waters behind the dam at Fries.*

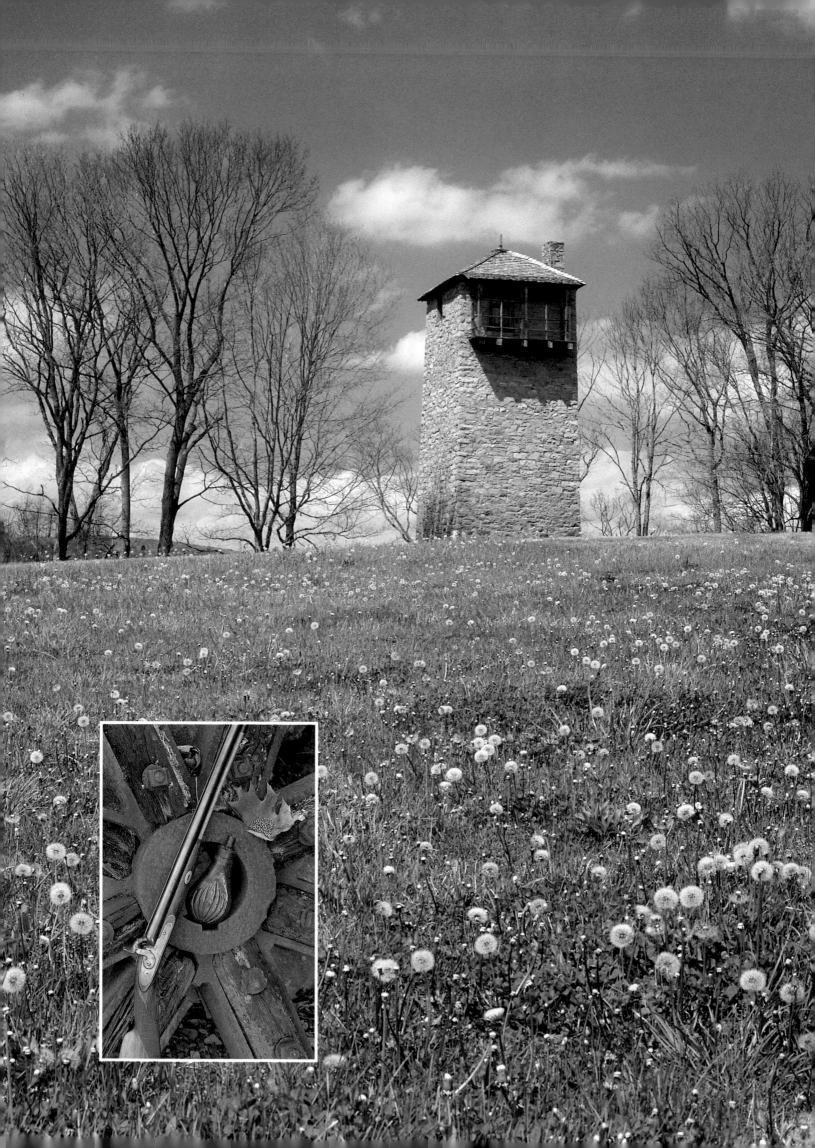

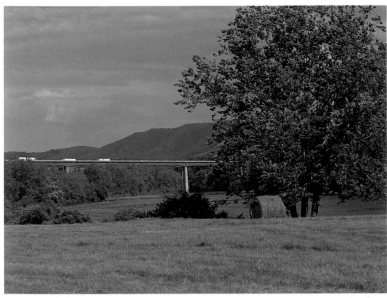

Arnout Hyde Jr.

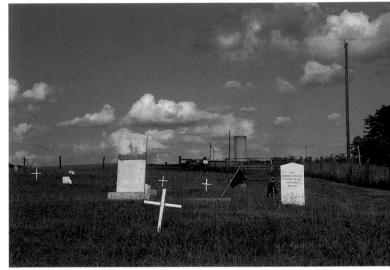

Top; *Interstate 77 crosses the New near the Shot Tower Historical State Park. Left; Shot tower that formed lead pellets. Left Insert; Old muzzle-loading shotgun that used pellets made by a shot tower. Right; Cemetery near Popular Camp where Confederate soldiers are buried. Perhaps these soldiers carried lead bullets mined from the Austinville mines. Right Below; Lead mine at Austinville.*

Arnout Hyde Jr.

SHOT TOWER HISTORICAL STATE PARK

Lead is a soft, silvery, malleable heavy metal, ideal for the bullets and shot used in yesterday's muzzleloading guns. Two methods were commonly used to form these lead balls. Either molten lead was poured into a mold to make the projectile, or molten lead was poured through a screen at the top of a shot tower. As goblets of lead fell in the tower, they would harden into spheres.

Thomas Jackson, an Englishman, migrated to Austinville, Virginia about 1785, and became associated with the lead mines discovered by Colonel Chiswell in 1756. Having become part owner of the mines, he constructed a shot tower so that a portion of the lead mined could be profitably sold as a finished product. Hunting needs made a ready market for the shot.

During the Civil War, these mines were the chief domestic supply of lead for the Confederacy; however, the lead balls made at the Tower were not used in the war, but only for hunting.

The Tower was built about 1807, with a base 20 feet square, 75 feet high and with a 75-foot vertical shaft below the Tower. Kettles of lead were melted at the top of the Tower and poured through various size screens, depending on the size pellet needed. The goblets of lead fell 150 feet through the Tower and shaft into a vessel of water. An access horizontal tunnel at the river's edge was connected to the bottom of the shaft. This access tunnel served several purposes: one was to supply water to the container catching the falling lead pellets, and another was to provide easy access to retrieve the lead pellets.

The Tower was donated to the Commonwealth of Virginia by the Lead Mines Ruritan Club, and was opened to the public in 1968. In 1981, the Shot Tower was designated a National Historic Mechanical Engineering Landmark by the American Society of Mechanical Engineers.

The Tower can be reached by U.S. Route 52, near where the highway crosses the New River in Wythe County, or by turning off the Poplar Camp Exit on Interstate 77.

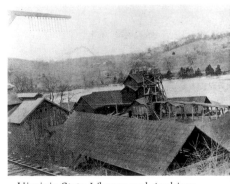

Virginia State Library and Archives

Gerald S. Ratliff

Insert; Arnout Hyde Jr.

NAVIGATING THE NEW RIVER IN VIRGINIA

The New River is the largest white-water river in Virginia that can be canoed year-round. Most rapids are classed according to difficulty, I through IV during normal flows, between spring and fall. Higher flows and cold weather increase these ratings, making the river dangerous to run, except by expert whitewater paddlers. A series of dams require difficult portages.

This river in Virginia offers excellent scenery, beautiful farm country, towering cliffs and interesting geological formations. Good fishing is also found in the river.

The general characteristics from the town, Mouth of Wilson to Claytor Lake, are: gradient, 5 feet per mile; average width 500 feet; length, 78 miles with 10 major rapids. From Claytor Lake to Bluestone Lake, the gradient is also 5 feet per mile, average width 550 feet, length 80 miles and also 10 major rapids.

There are a number of outfitters that supply organized trips with rental canoes, and camping facilities for the New River in Virginia.

Right; *Aerial view of rapids below Byllesby Dam, ideal for open boat white water canoeing.* Below; *Couple enjoys floating the river.*

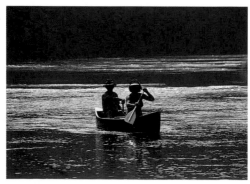

Stephen J. Shaluta Jr.

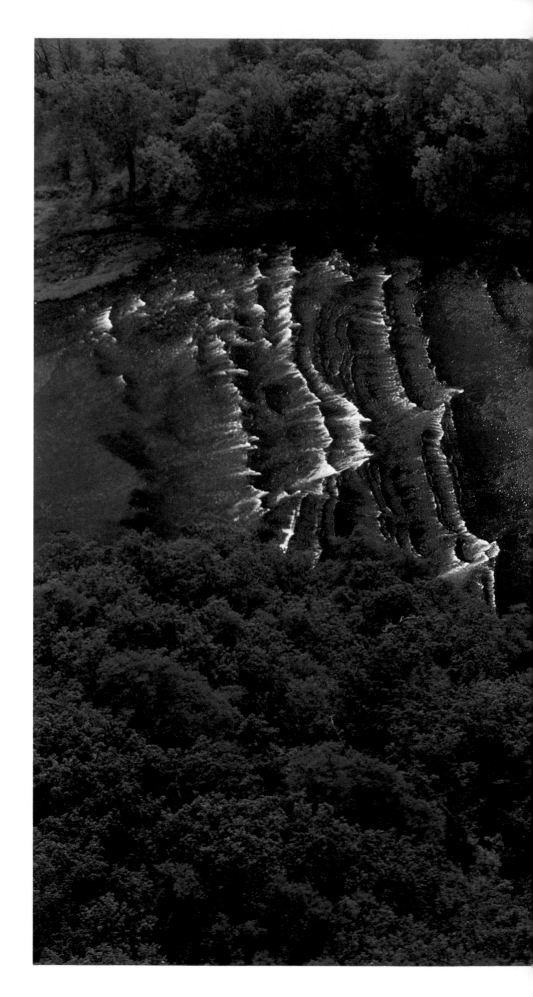

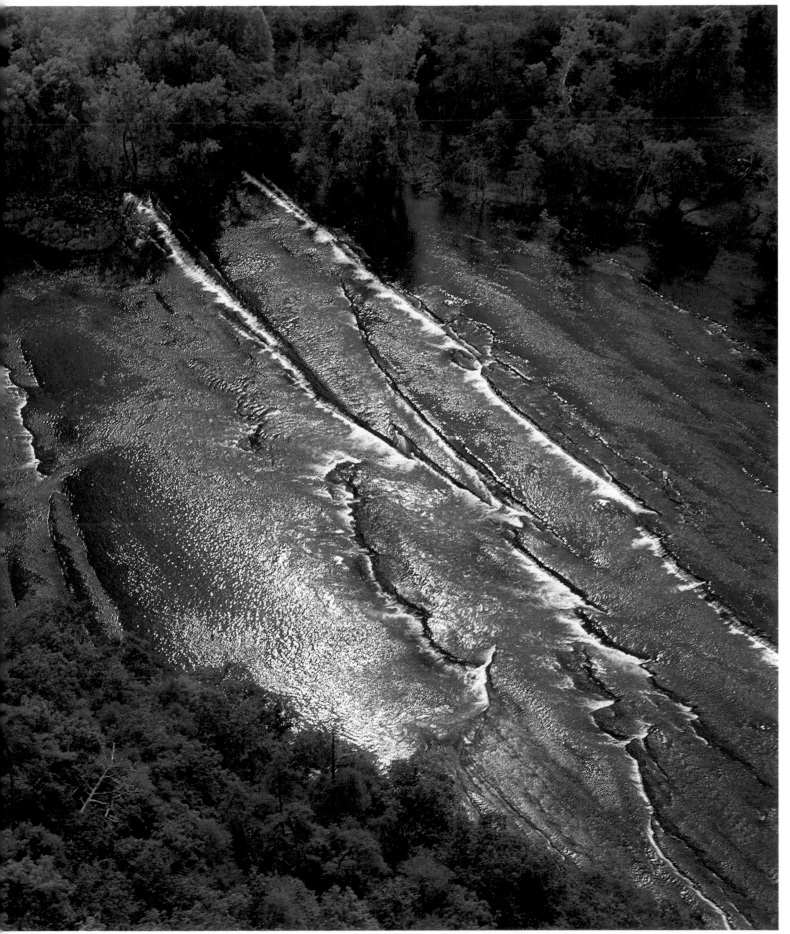

Arnout Hyde Jr.

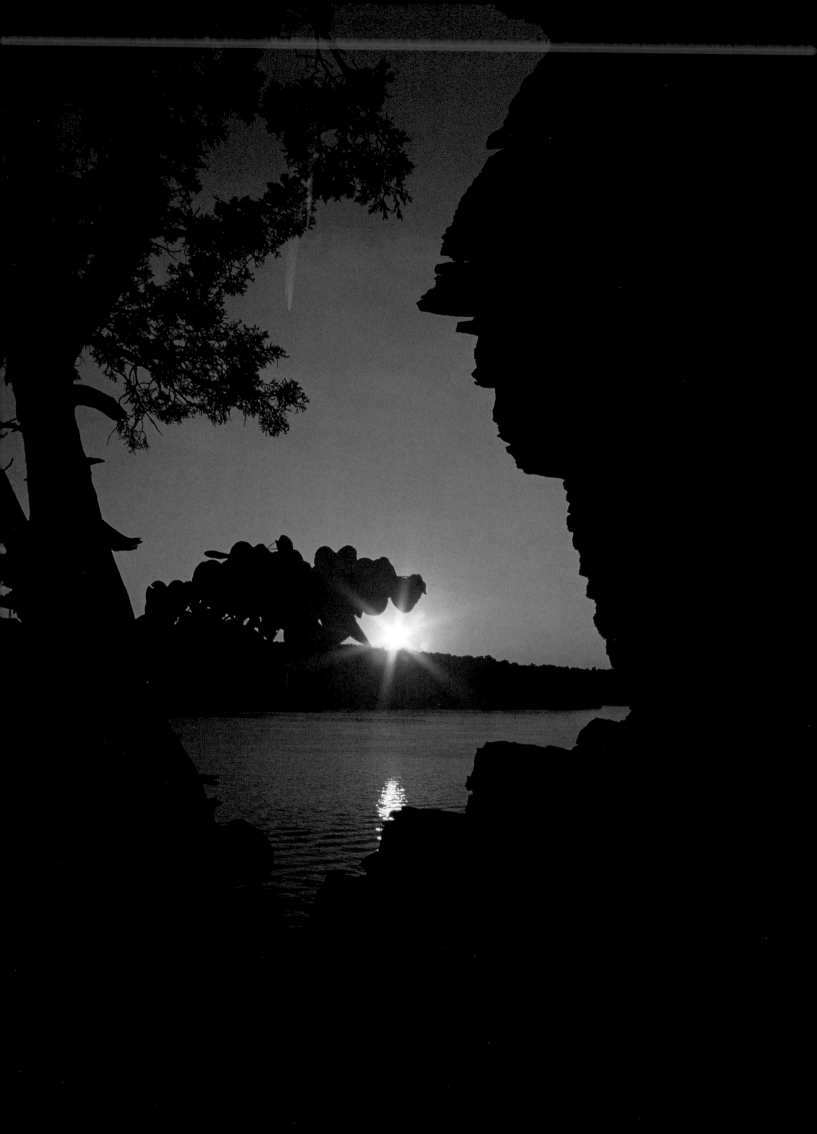

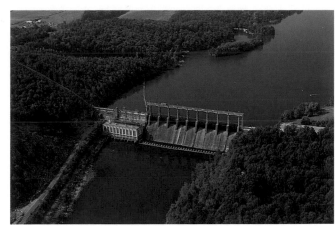

Aerial view of Claytor Lake dam.

CLAYTOR LAKE

Sunset from Overlook Trail at Claytor Lake.

Claytor Dam was completed in 1939 by the Appalachian Power Company at a cost of eleven million dollars. Its purpose is to generate electricity. The dam has created a 4,500-acre lake, 21 miles long with 101 miles of wooded shoreline. A 472-acre state park, Claytor Lake State Park, is located along these shores. The powerhouse at the dam has 4 generating units, with a capacity of 75,000 K.W. Dimensions of the dam are: 1,150 feet long, 130 feet high, with a thickness of 108 feet at the base.

The park and lake are located 2 miles southeast of Interstate 81 (Exit 33) on State Route 660. The park's visitor's center is in the Howe House built in 1876–79. Water sports are popular, with boating, water skiing and fishing as favorites. A sandy beach has a bathhouse and lifeguard on duty during the summer. The park offers 4 campgrounds, 12 housekeeping cabins and 136 tent camping spots. A full-service marina is available for boaters. Four trails are open year-round.

The entire Claytor Lake complex is a balance of private needs for land ownership for homes and public needs for outdoor recreation.

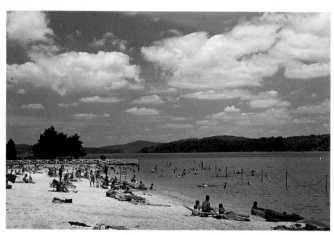

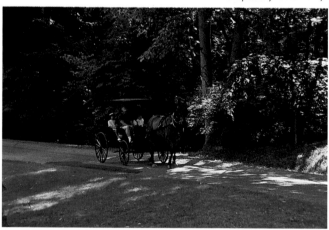

Top; *Swimmers enjoy the white sand beach at Claytor Lake.* Right; *Water-skier David Strenz makes a graceful turn in the lake.* Above; *A family enjoys a horse-drawn carriage ride offered at Claytor Lake State Park.*

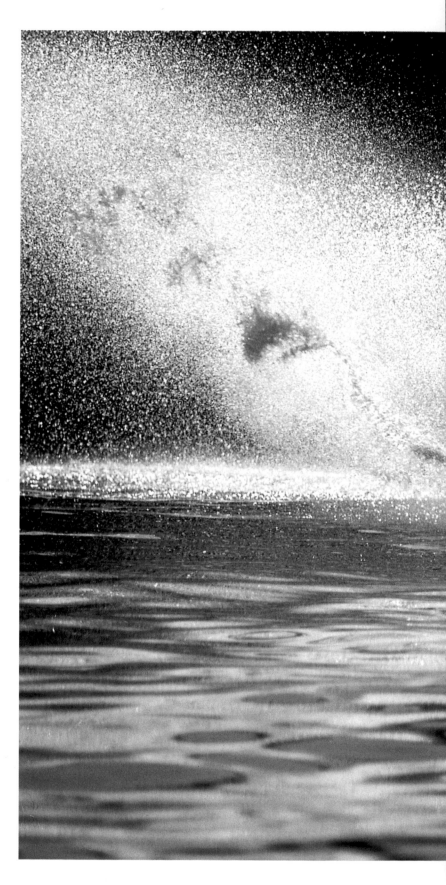

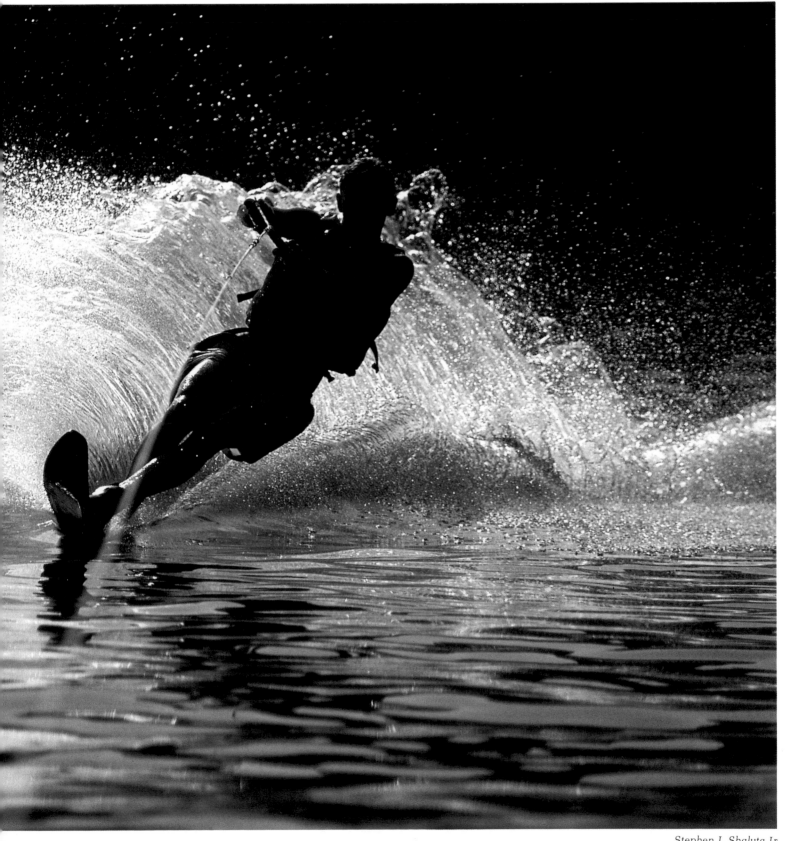

Stephen J. Shaluta Jr.

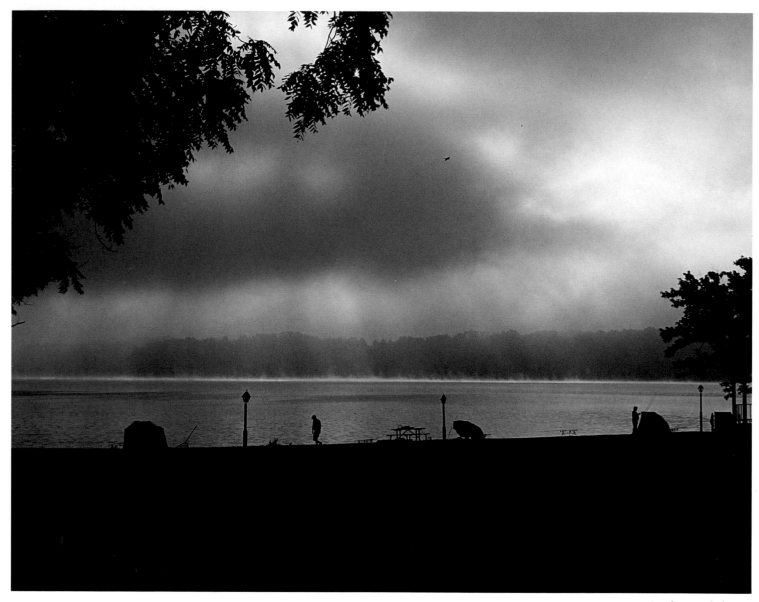

Stephen J. Shaluta Jr.

Morning sun rays welcome fisherman at Claytor.

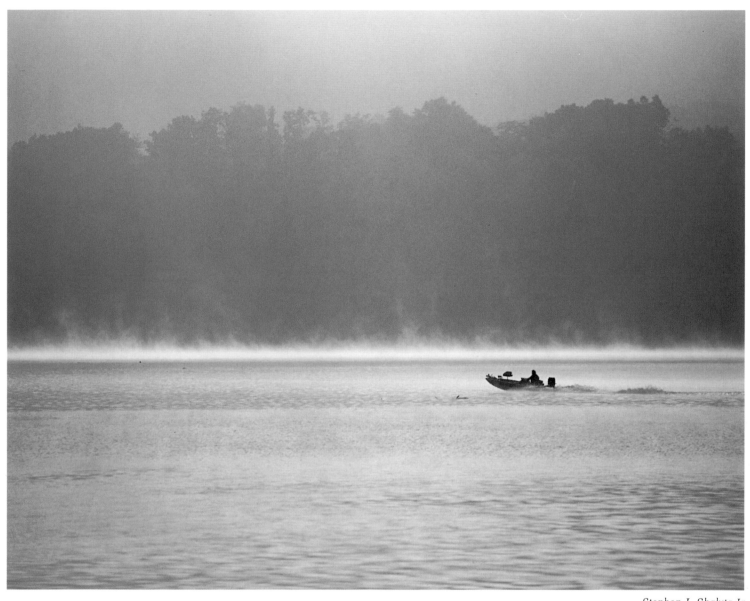

A boat glides along the lake with an early-rising morning mist.

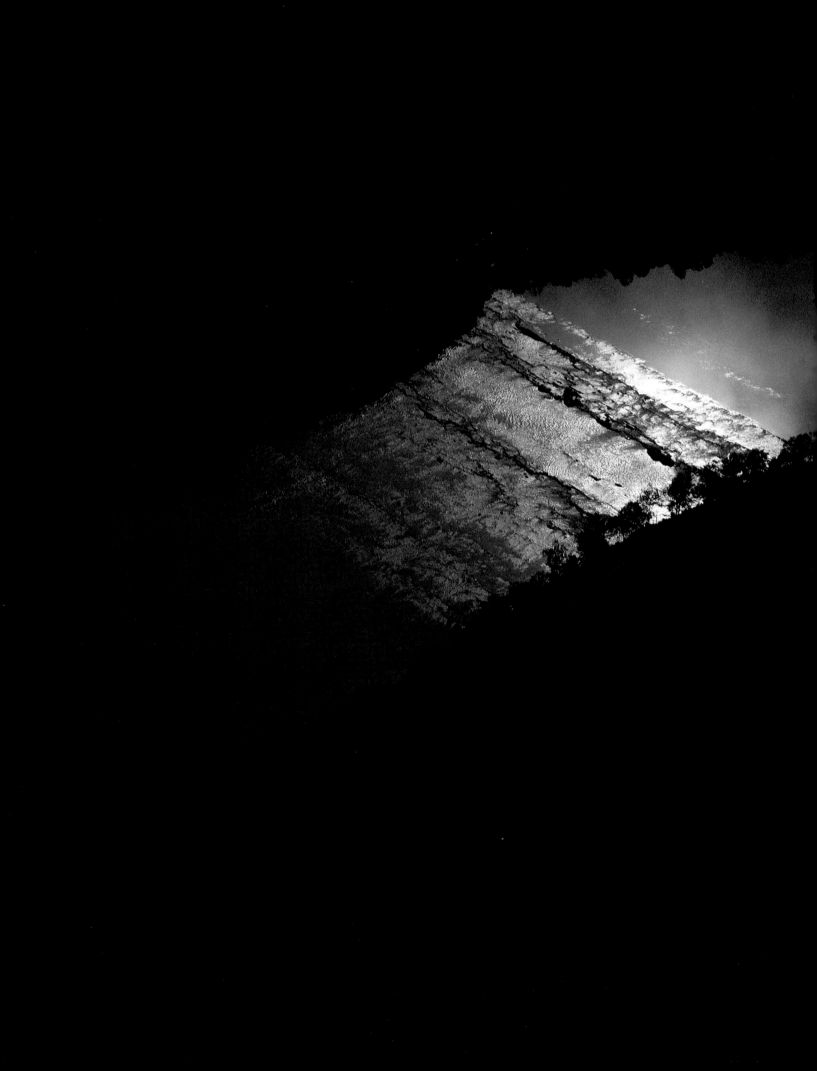

CLAYTOR LAKE
TO BLUESTONE LAKE

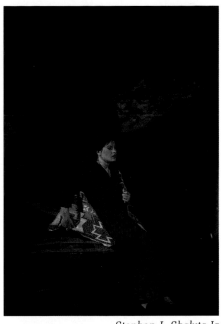

Stephen J. Shaluta Jr.
A scene from the drama "The Long Way Home," depicting the Mary Ingles story.

The waters surge from Claytor Lake passing Radford, the largest town on the New River. The town started as a ferry stop years ago, and enticed businesses, industries and a railroad. In 1930, Radford was chosen for a federal arsenal. During World War II, 20,000 employees made explosives. The Hercules Arsenal, the largest employer in the region, is still a large, viable industry.

Radford University, located on the banks of the New River, is a four-year, medium-size, state-supported university. The beautiful 154-acre campus is bounded to the west by the city of Radford. The school has approximately 9000 students, while the population of the town is 14,000.

The river has an early frontier history steeped in drama and violence. With the settlement of the region by European immigrants, conflicts were aroused with bands of marauding Indians. Perhaps the most famous story is that of Mary Draper Ingles, a courageous woman captured by Indians, and her escape and tortuous return to the area. During June through September, the saga "The Long Way Home" is reenacted in the Ingles Homestead Amphitheater, the actual location of her homesite and grave.

After the river passes through the Heart of Virginia's New River Valley, it makes a dramatic cut through the mountains called the Narrows. It is not far from here at Rich Creek that the second largest diamond in North America was found.

From the air, one can see a series of horseshoe curves with impressive cliffs abound with railroad tracks parallelling this stretch of the river on both sides. The river is quite wide through the valley, and narrows down through the cuts in the mountains. Ledges of rocks create nice rapids, ideal for whitewater canoeing.

This segment of the river, with its tranquil valley and beautiful mountain cuts, is a tribute to a past odyssey of a courageous woman's journey "a Long Way Home."

The sunlight gives a golden cast to an aerial view of a rapid near the Narrows.

rnout Hyde Jr.

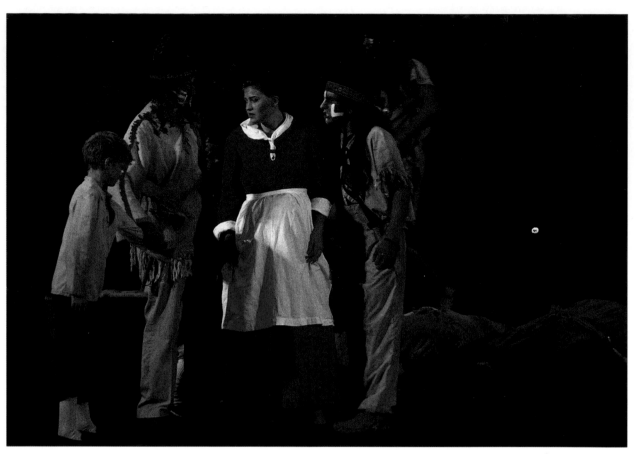

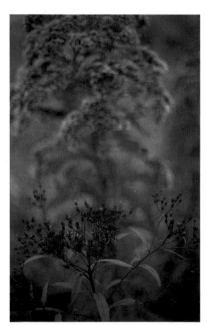

Arnout Hyde Jr.

Top; *Scene from the drama "The Long Way Home." Above; A symbolic composition of flowers—how Mary Ingles must have felt from the elements ready to seize her.*

THE MARY INGLES SAGA

The Mary Draper Ingles saga is an example of one woman's outstanding courage, endurance and determination to escape from her Indian captors and return home.

The Ingles family was living at Draper's meadow when it was attacked by Shawnee Indians on July 8, 1755. Everyone present in the community was either killed, wounded or seized. Mary's husband, William, was away from home at the time. Mary and two young sons were captured and taken to an Indian town on the Ohio River. During the three-day journey, Mary gave birth to a baby girl. Mary and an "old Dutch woman," captured in Pennsylvania, were taken to Kentucky to make salt, in an area near where Cincinnati is now located.

Mary and the Dutch woman, Mrs. Dunn, made plans to escape, leaving the baby girl with the Indians. They followed the Ohio River on the Kentucky side to above the Big Sandy River where they crossed on driftwood. They followed the south side of the Kanawha River to the Coal River. After a tortuous journey, they came to the mouth of the Bluestone River. Throughout the trip, they were on a starvation diet, subsisting on nuts, berries and roots. At this point, the Dutch lady became mad, threatening to kill and eat Mary. The two continued their journey, but on opposite sides of the river. Mary was found by Adam Harmon in the Giles County area of the New River, and returned home. A search party found the Dutch woman and returned her to Pennsylvania.

Mary and William resumed their lives together and had four more children. Of the captured sons, George died in captivity; Thomas was ransomed and returned home 13 years later at the age of 17.

William died in 1782 at the age of 53, and Mary died at the age of 83.

The incredible Mary Ingles story is dramatized annually as "The Long Way Home," which is entering its 20th season. The play is performed in an amphitheater located at Radford, Virginia, one-fourth mile from Exit 34 off Interstate 81.

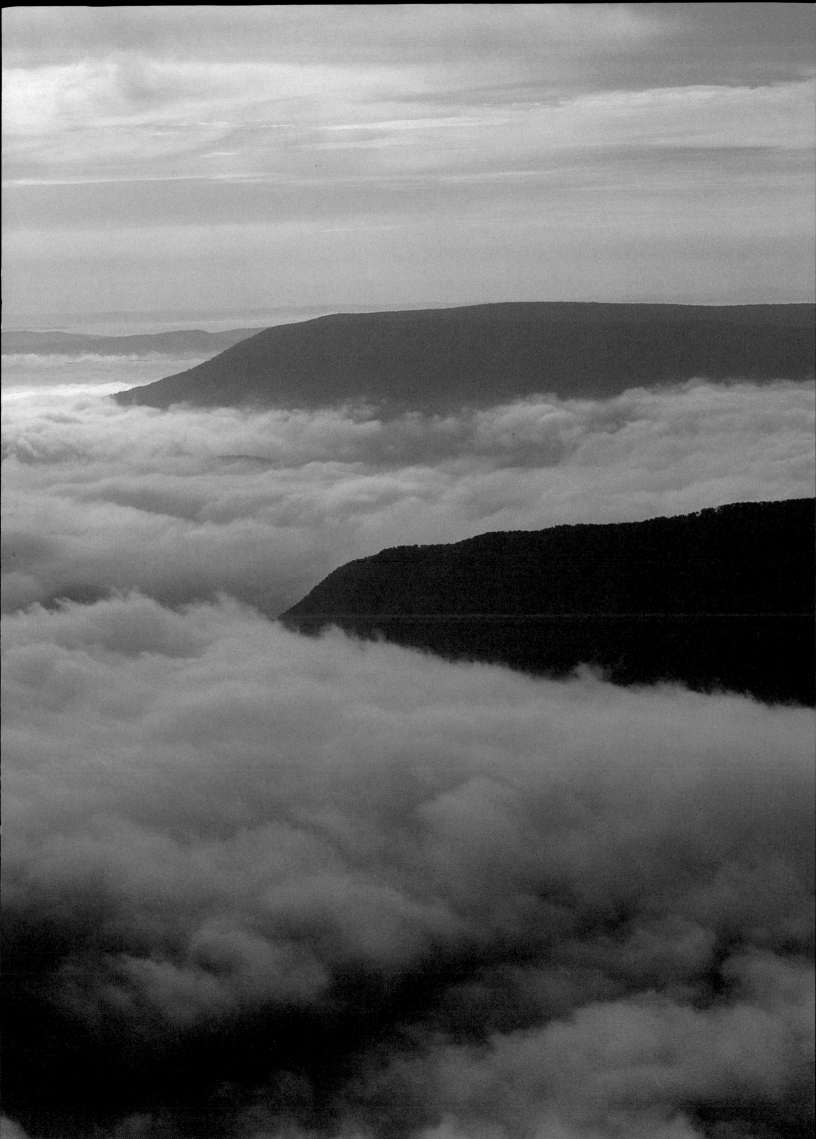

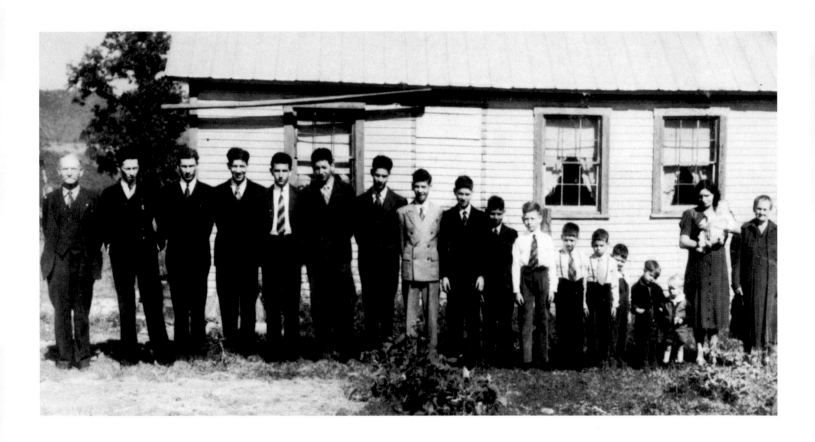

HORSESHOE DIAMOND

Grover, Father (far left), and Annie, Mother (far right). The first 16 of the 17 children were boys, a world's record for consecutive male births. Child in Mother's arms is the only girl. William "Punch" Jones, second from left, found the diamond while pitching horseshoes

One of the most interesting stories told along the New River includes a diamond, a game of horseshoes and a family with 17 children.

Annie and Grover Jones lived with their 17 children at Peterstown along Rich Creek, a tributary to the New River. The first 16 children were boys, which set a world's record for consecutive male births, as recorded in Ripley's "Believe It or Not." This unusual story begins in 1928. The oldest son, William (Punch), was pitching horseshoes with his father. While retrieving a horseshoe, he caught a glimpse of a glass-like stone. That evening he dropped the stone into a cheese box with some tools, where it was all but forgotten for many years.

With the outbreak of World War II, Punch took a job at an army ammunition plant where he worked with carbons. He remembered the stone in the cheese box, and contemplated the possibilities of its being a diamond, since diamonds are composed entirely of carbon. Returning home, he retrieved the almost forgotten stone, and successfully scratched a window pane with it. Believing it to be a diamond, he had Professor R. J. Holden, professor of geology at Virginia Poly-technic Institute, examine the stone. Professor Holden's tests proved conclusively this was an alluvial diamond, weighing 34.46 carats and having a diameter of 5/8 inch. Sometimes nicknamed the Horseshoe Diamond, it was the only diamond found in West Virginia and the second largest found in the United States. Geologists believe that glaciers during the Ice Age deposited the few isolated diamonds found in America.

The story turns to a sad event on Easter Sunday in 1945. Punch lost his life as a valiant soldier in the Battle of the Bulge in Germany. Through the luck of a horseshoe, the finder never gained any financial reward for his discovery.

This gem was displayed at the Smithsonian Institution from 1944 until 1968. Grover Jones returned the stone to West Virginia and it went on display at the state fair.

The story continues with still another mystery. Annie Jones remembered that when she was a child, her aunt told her of finding glass or shiny peebles which resembled diamonds in Rich Creek. Could these have been what Punch found? Perhaps, but hundreds of people have searched the area for these elusive gems to no avail.

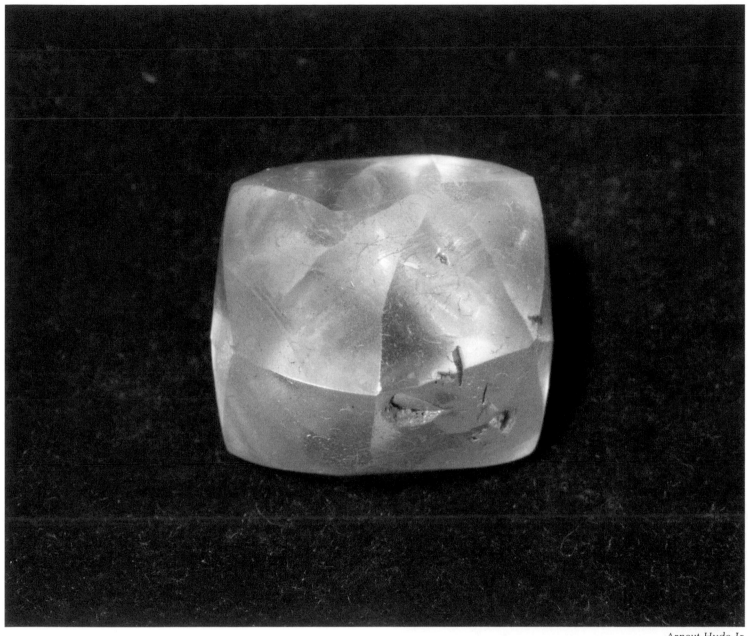

Top; *The Horseshoe Diamond.* Right; *Aerial view of Peterstown and Rich Creek where the Horseshoe Diamond was found.*

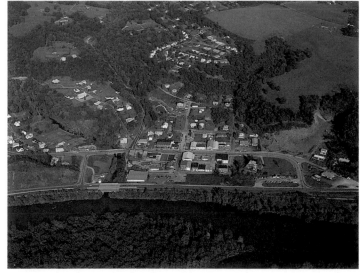

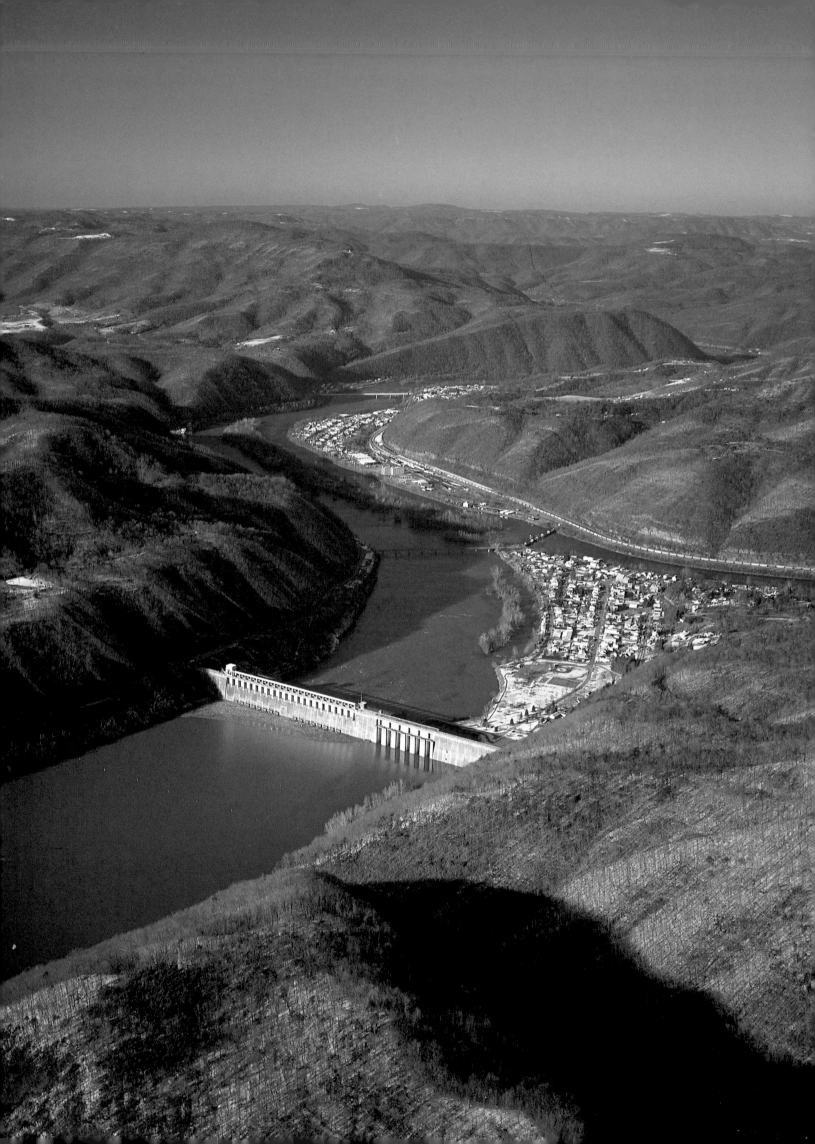

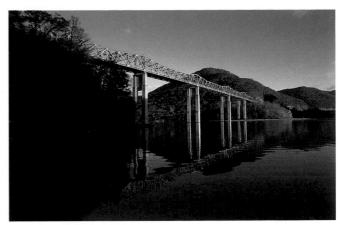

Route 20 crosses over a part of Bluestone Lake at Bluestone State Park.

BLUESTONE LAKE

Winter aerial view of Bluestone Dam with the New River and Hinton in the background.

The Bluestone Dam and Lake, built by the Corps of Engineers, was started in March, 1942, but was halted during the war years. The project was completed in December, 1948. Bluestone is one of a network of projects built by the Corps to control disastrous flooding of the Kanawha and Ohio rivers. The precipitous West Virginia terrain allows rapid runoff of deluge rainfall conditions which are now stored in the flood control lakes and later released under control.

In addition to flood control, the lakes furnish important recreational facilities. Bluestone Lake covers 1,800 acres and is the third largest in West Virginia. Boating, fishing, camping and hiking trails are available and frequently used. Crappie, bluegills, bass and catfish are the varieties of fish most commonly caught.

Bluestone State Park adjoining the lake has a 20,000-acre public hunting and fishing area. There are rental cabins, an administration and recreation building, and several campgrounds. The area is complete with all the facilities one expects to find in a West Virginia state park.

The name Bluestone derives from the layers of bluish-gray shale among the reddish sandstone present in the area.

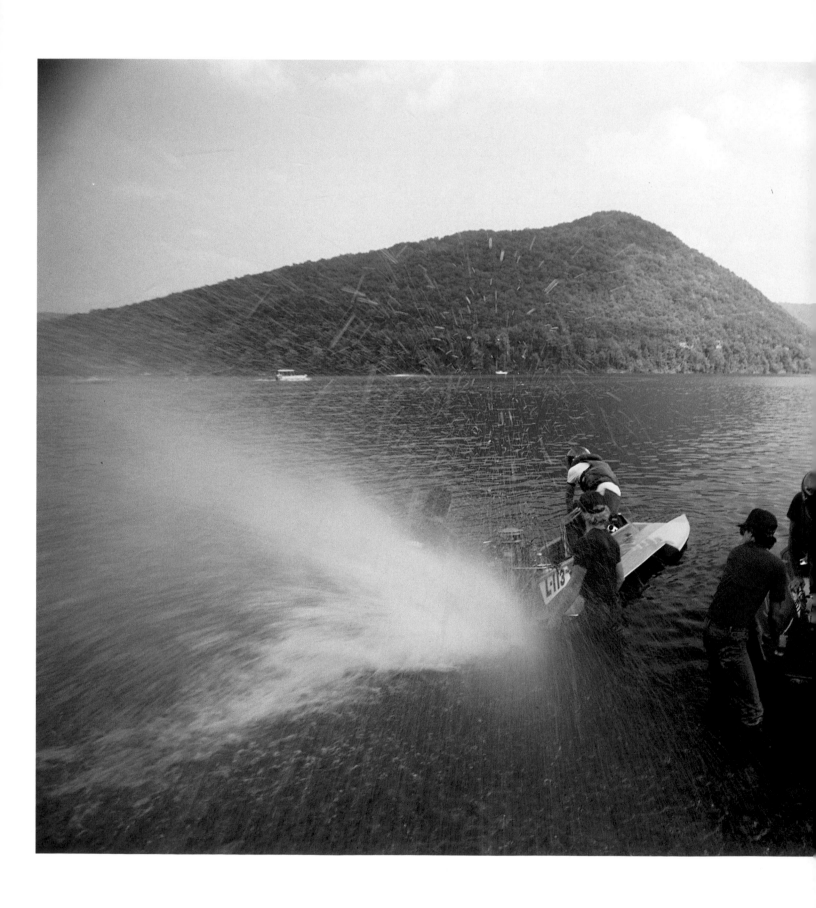

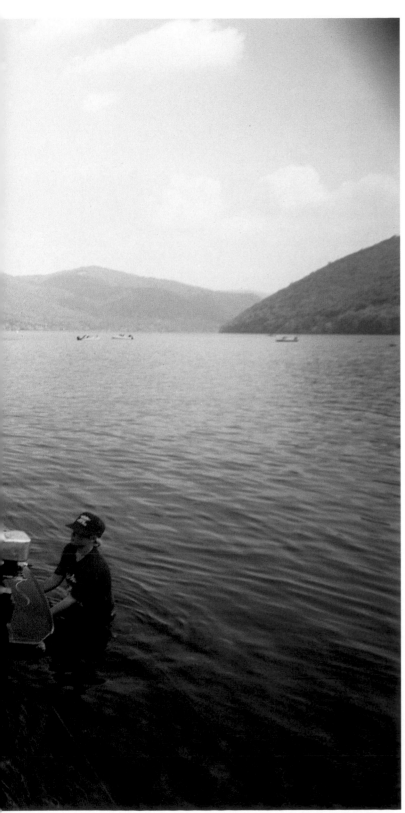

Left; *Power boat races on Bluestone Lake during the West Virginia Water Festival at Hinton. Below; Autumn view of Bluestone Lake State Park. Overleaf; Late summer scene of Bluestone Lake.*

Overleaf; Arnout Hyde Jr.

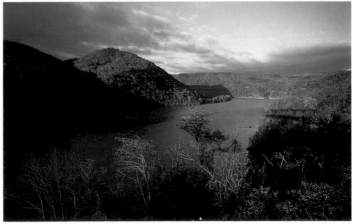

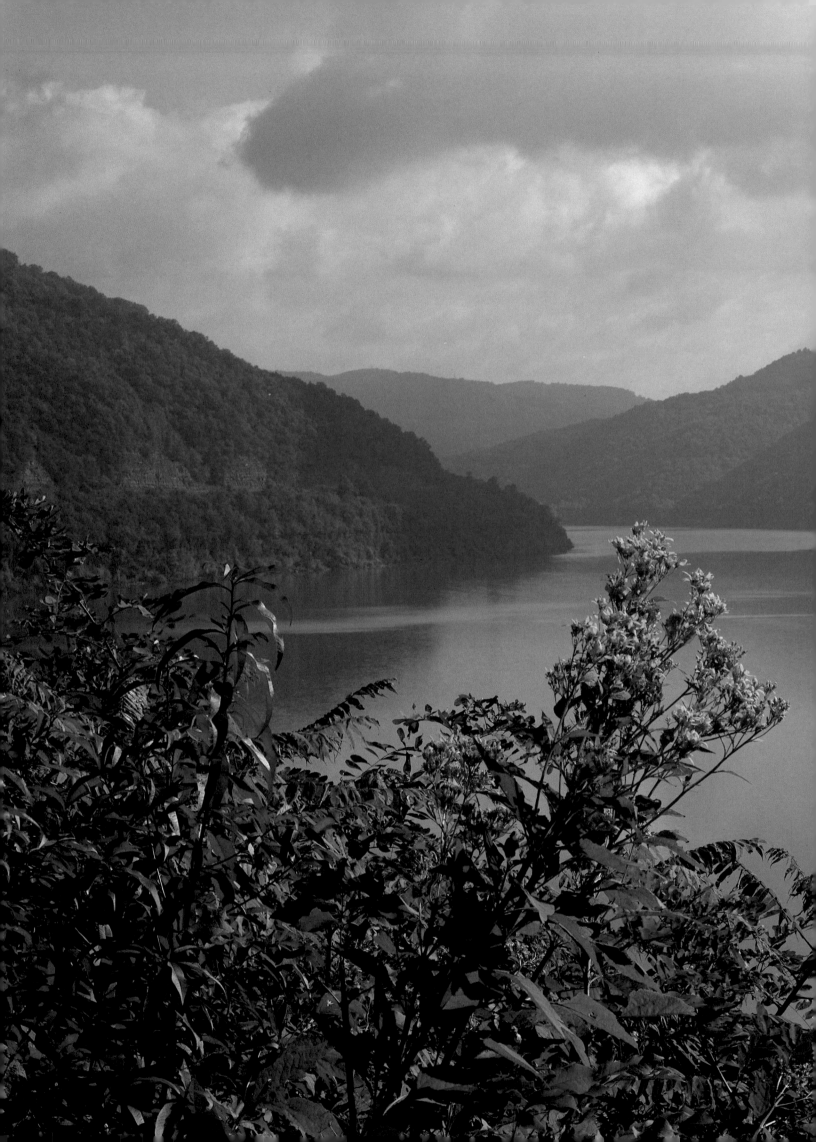

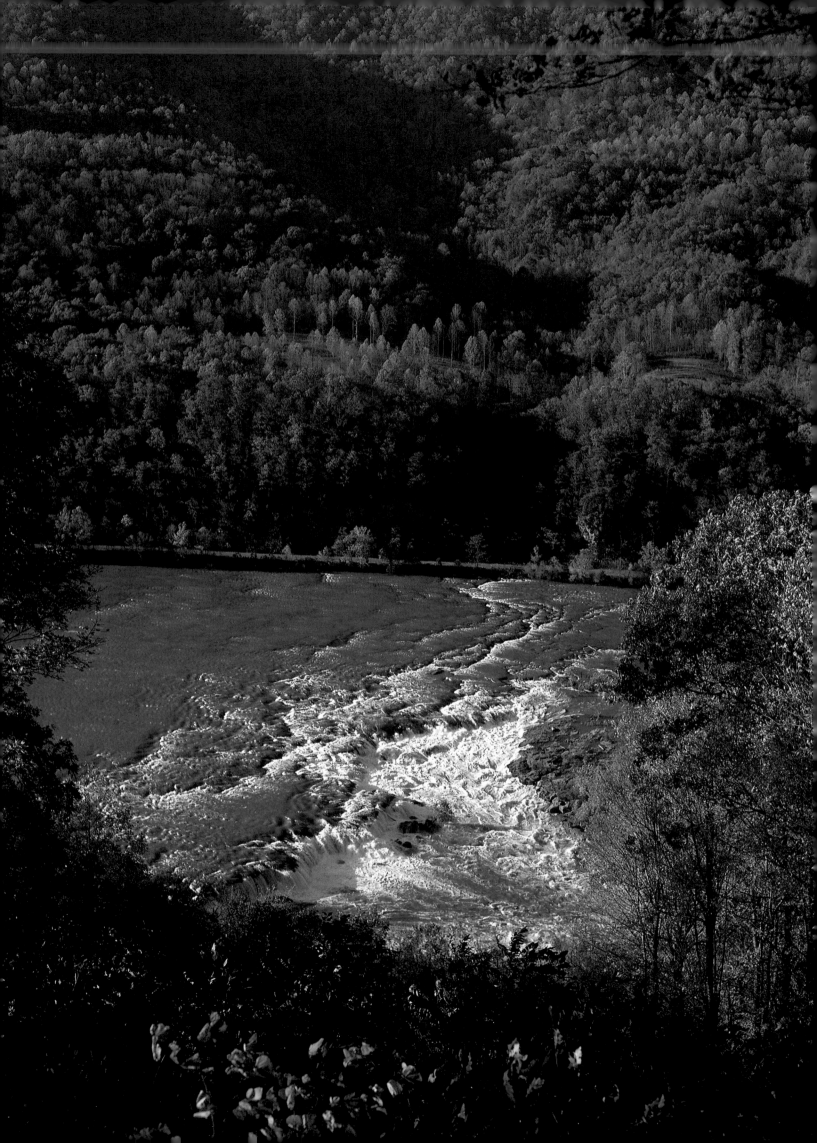

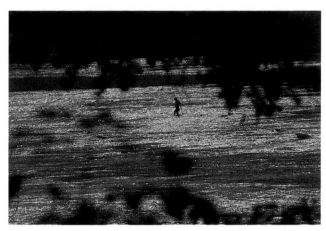

A fisherman seines for minnows at dusk, below the Bluestone Dam.

BLUESTONE

TO THURMOND

A gargantuan concrete dam upriver from Hinton holds back millions of gallons of water, although some is released through gates that roar over the spillway creating a fine mist of spray. These waters spread quickly across the rocky river bed that welcomes thousands of fishermen each year. Wading or taking boats close to the spillway rewards anglers with some of the finest fishing on the New. The two major tributaries that flow into the New are in this area: Greenbrier River below the Bluestone Dam and the Bluestone River into Bluestone Lake.

Hinton is the only major town on the river in West Virginia. This is unusual since most rivers of this size have towns lining their banks. Hinton became a town of importance in 1873 when the C&O railway line was completed. The railroad brought prosperity, and at one time 14 passenger trains stopped daily. This fine old river railroad town with its wonderful people each fall welcomes passengers from the Collis P. Huntington Railroad Historical Society's Steam Excursion by holding a street fair of arts and crafts exhibits, food and entertainment.

The New River Gorge National River begins at Hinton with its interesting history of once-thriving mining and lumber communities along its course. A point of interest as the river flows north is Sandstone Falls, named after a nearby rock quarry that supplied sandstone for the building of the Washington Monument. The National Park Service has built boardwalks to the falls so that all can view this magnificent cataract. The river passes by formerly prosperous areas that flourished at the turn of the century. At one time, colorful names such as Quinnimont, Terry, Thayer and Grandview marked the map. The McKendree Hospital once treated miners and trained nurses in the southern part of the state. Now just old foundations remain as a reminder of an era past.

The mountains begin to hug the river as it proceeds north with a few fields here and there which supported an occasional farm along the floodplains. Long stretches of flat water are interrupted with intermediate rapids, making this a popular region for family rafting and fishing.

Autumn view of Sandstone Falls.

Arnout Hyde Jr.

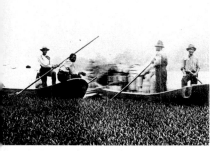

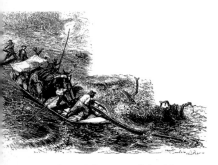

Top; *Bateau boats on the New River - date and locations unknown.* Above; *The book THE SOUTHERN STATES OF NORTH AMERICA published 1874 tells of boatmen plying the New River Canyon in a 60-foot bateau - which could be hired to go down the gorge. An artist made the above sketch on one such trip in 1873. Opposite Page; Sandstone Falls, one of the difficult areas the bateau boats had to be taken around the falls.*

THE FIRST BOAT TRAVEL IN THE GORGE

It is difficult to imagine that on a mist-covered morning in July, 1869 one would have seen a 50-foot bateau boat negotiating the dangerous rapids in the gorge, but such a trip may have occurred. While researching material in the West Virginia Archive for this book, co-author Gerald Ratliff found the following account in the newspaper, THE WEST VIRGINIA JOURNAL, dated September 11, 1869.

A WONDERFUL ADVENTURE—NEW RIVER NAVIGATED

Mr. James R. Dempsey of Fayette County, W.Va. furnishes us with the following: On the 10th, he in the company with five others started from the Falls of Kanawha with a bateau, 50 feet long, 8 feet wide and 23 inches deep (having a few days before taken it up over the Falls on rollers) and went up New River over rocks and rapids and around its deep bends, through its awful gorges, up and up, ascending many feet to the mile, until they reached Townells Ferry, where they got two more hands to assist them, when they proceeded on up the river to Bowyer's Ferry, a distance of about 35 miles, at which place the boat was left for the use of the C.&O. R.R., at whose instance the adventure was made. The distance of 35 miles was made in six days, having an average of about 6 miles per day.

We regard this adventure as the only successful one that has ever yet been made over that awfully grand river and much credit is due Mr. Dempsey and crew for their untiring energy in making an accomplishment of the adventure, the first on record.

He informed us that the river is much worse than it is commonly understood to be, as every few hundred yards they encountered perpendicular falls, varying from 2 to 4 feet high, and that it was common thing to pass up slopes 4 to 7 feet perpendicular. This is a remarkable, and we give names of the gentleman who first ascended it by boat; J.W. Dempsey, commander, J.R. Dempsey, H.R. Dempsey, O.W. Dempsey, E.

Nowgin, H. Martin, J. Rodea and A. Rodea.

Another account from the biography of General Huntington describes a similar bateau boat, built under the direction of William Hinton, traveling from Hinton to Kanawha Falls in July, 1869. River men were hired at $10 to pole the craft with a party of distinguished gentlemen, namely, Collis P. Huntington, Colonel Delos W. Emmons, Major H.D. Whitcomb, and General John Echols. Undoubtedly, this was the same bateau boat James R. Dempsey brought up the river. The purpose of the trip was to investigate a proposed route for the C&O railroad. Interestingly, not only did the trip come down the river, but the boat was poled and dragged up the New—an usual feat even by today's standards.

Another account of a trip from the JOURNAL OF THE HOUSE OF DELEGATES OF THE COMMONWEALTH OF VIRGINIA dated 1812, was a journey down the Gorge, investigating a possible James River and New River Canal. The trip was made by Chief Justice John Marshall.

The boat which conveyed your Commisioners, passed from the mouth of Greenbrier, to the place where their expedition terminated, without being taken out of the water, except at the Great Falls of the New River (Sandstone Falls), and at the Great Falls of the Kanawha. It was in the usual way through all the other difficult places which abound in New River, except two—both below Bowyer's Ferry. Through these it was conducted by ropes.

The boat was not laden, nor was it empty. In addition to the number of hands usually employed in navigation, it carried between two and three thousand weight.

It is also worthy of notice, that this voyage was performed by boatmen who, having never seen the river, were reduced to the necessity of selecting their way at the moment, without the aid of previous information.

Considerably more information is contained in this account; however, space does not permit the reprinting of it here.

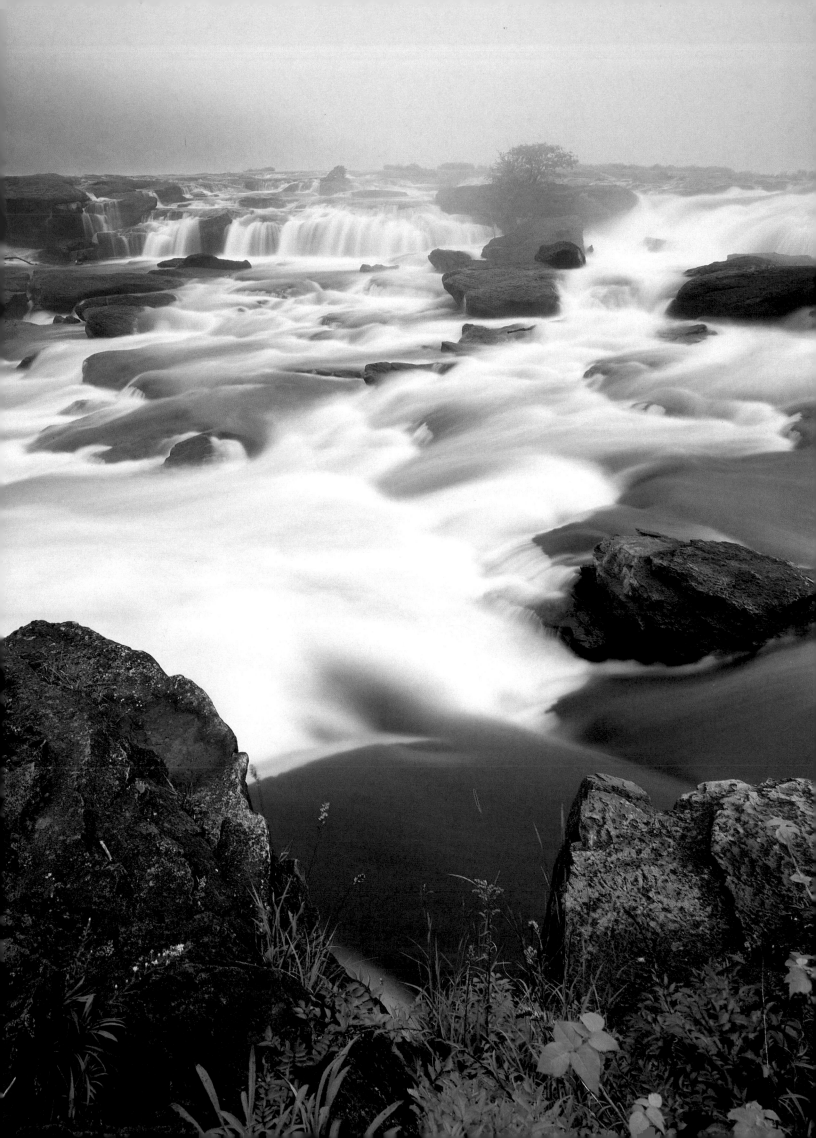

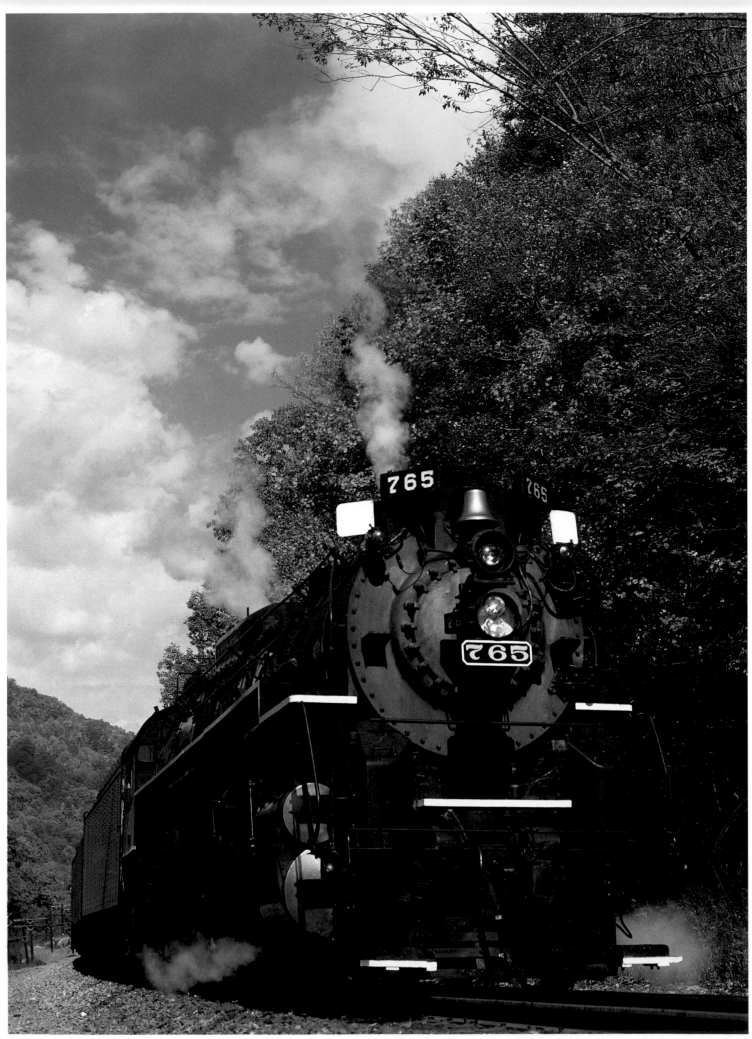

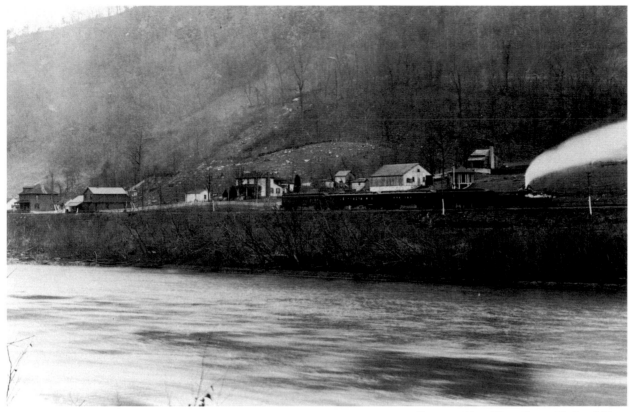

Top; *Steam train passes by Prince. Date unknown.* Left; *Steam locomotive, sponsored by the Collis P. Huntington Railroad Historical Society, pulls coaches during the steam excursion along the New River.*

RAILROAD HISTORY ALONG THE NEW RIVER

In 1870, large gangs of both white and black workmen were employed to begin construction on the Chesapeake and Ohio Railroad between White Sulphur Springs and Huntington. The black crew started at White Sulphur Springs, while the white crew began at Huntington. Just a year earlier, Collis P. Huntington, with a distinguished group of gentlemen, traveled down the New River in a 50-foot bateau, surveying for a railroad route. The two construction crews met near Hawks Nest on January 27, 1873. The last spike was driven commemorating the completion of the C&O Railroad from Richmond to Huntington, a distance of 414 miles. During the construction, engineers claimed, "The best workmen anywhere in the world were those Negroes." A note of historical interest: four years earlier, another last spike was driven connecting the Central Pacific and Union Pacific, the transcontinental railroad in the west.

An interesting phase of the construction occurred at Hawks Nest. The cliffs along the river, where the railroad bed was to be, were a series of pillar rock cliffs, much different from now. At the time, they were named Marshall's Pillar, after Justice John Marshall. Hundreds of pounds of black powder were poured in a crevice behind these rock formations. A tremendous blast blew these cliffs into the New River, damming the river and backing it up for miles until it was cleared. This line of track opened the way for the many mining communities that soon developed. Trains carried coal, timber, freight, and passengers. Since 1966, the Collis P. Huntington Railroad Historical Society, the Chesapeake and Ohio Railroad, and CSX Corporation resurrected a steam engine and coaches for a train trip through the Gorge. The trip starts at Huntington, goes to Hinton, and then returns. These trips, made three times during October, offer photo opportunities in such railroad towns as Thurmond and Hinton. Many rail fans including Dewey Yates, President of the Collis P. Huntington Railroad Historical Society, Incorporated, consider this the premier steam excursion in America. Anyone interested in these trips may write C. P. Huntington Railroad Historical Society, P.O. Box 1252, Ashland, Kentucky 41105. Telephone information is available by calling (304) 522-6140 or (304) 768-4323.

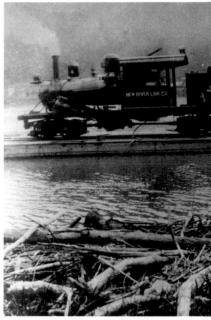

Thirty-five-ton Class B Climax being floated across New River to New River Lumber Co. in 1927.

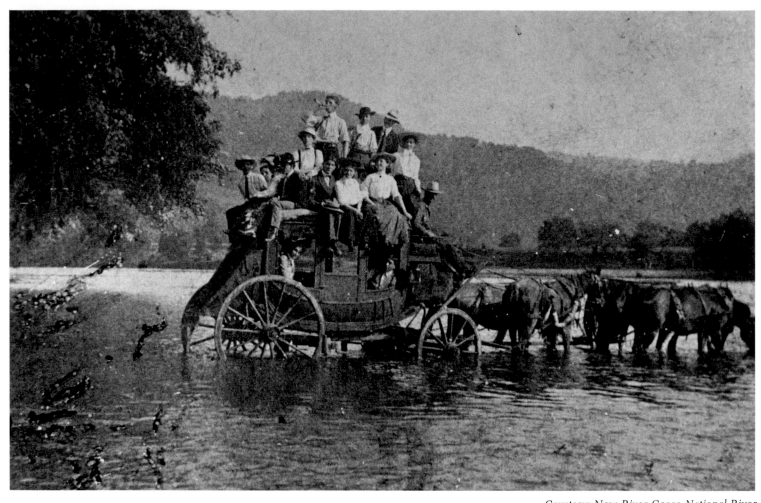

The railroad was not the only means of transportation along the
New River. This old photo, taken at Bellepoint on the New, dated
July 3, 1903, was titled "The Merry Coaching Party."

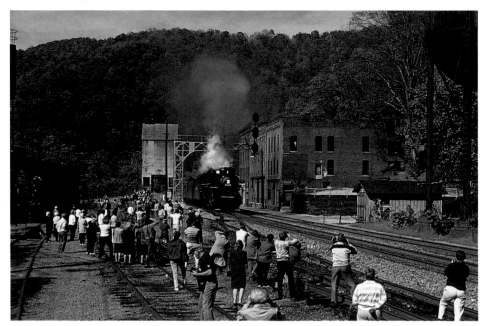

An interesting comparison; 1990
scene of the Former Nickel Plated
Road Engine No. 765 as it passes
through Thurmond during the New
River Steam Excursion. The same
type engine at the business section
of Thurmond some years past.

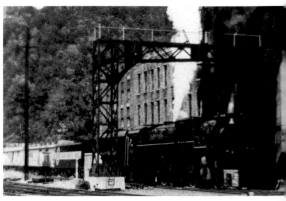

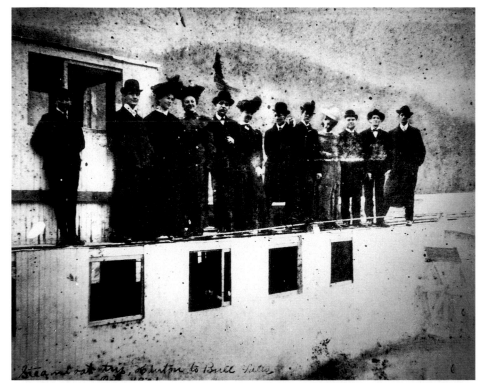

Courtesy; New River Gorge National River

Left; *While most steam power was utilized for the railroad, this form of energy also moved a steamboat from Hinton to Bull Falls. This photo was dated Oct. 1906. Supposedly, the boat sank and is still on the bottom of the river. Below; Aerial of Hinton, an important railroad town in southern West Virginia, during the 1990 steam excursion on the New River.*

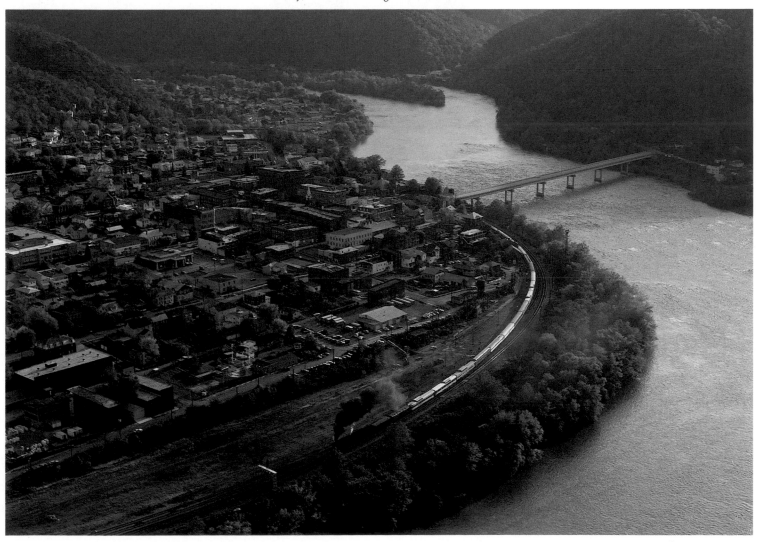

Arnout Hyde Jr.

53

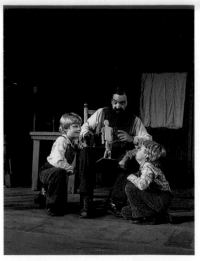

Arnout Hyde Jr.

GRANDVIEW

In 1855, Joseph Carper, a well-known gunsmith, settled along the rim of the New River Gorge. He called the area "Grandview" for the spectacular view of the Gorge. A community with that name was later established there.

The State of West Virginia, in 1939, purchased 52 acres from a coal company to form a State park as a day use area. The park offers overlooks, picnic areas, playgrounds and hiking trails. An outdoor amphitheater features dramas in the summer. "Honey in The Rock" is a play telling the story of how West Virginia became a State during the Civil War. This production is one of the longest running outdoor dramas in the country, starting in the late 1960s. On alternate summer evenings, the drama "Hatfields and McCoys" tells the history of the famous family feud in southern West Virginia and Kentucky over ownership of a pig.

Catawba Rhododendron bloom during May each year with thousands of blossoms throughout the park, and impressive stands among the cliffs overlooking the river. This showy display of rhododendron, whose natural habitat is in North Carolina and Tennessee, found its way down the New River, propagating areas along the way.

The National Park Service recently incorporated this State park into the New River National River. Plans are being made to build an Appalachian Heritage Center, which will exhibit regional folk art and will also sponsor workshops featuring crafts and music of the area. This complex will be a showcase for the region.

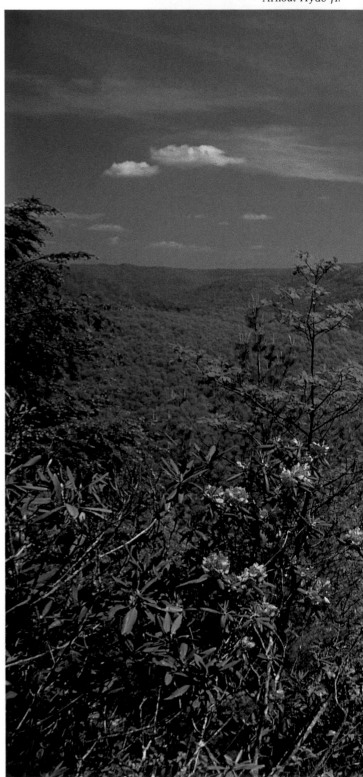

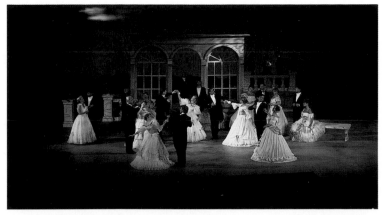

Left; Scene from the outdoor drama "Honey in the Rock" at Grandview Amphitheater. Far Left; Scene from "Hatfields and McCoys." Below; Catawba Rhododendron in bloom at the Grandview Park overlook. Overleaf; Morning fog fills the valley seen from Grandview Park's main overlook.   Overleaf; Arnout Hyde Jr.

Arnout Hyde Jr.

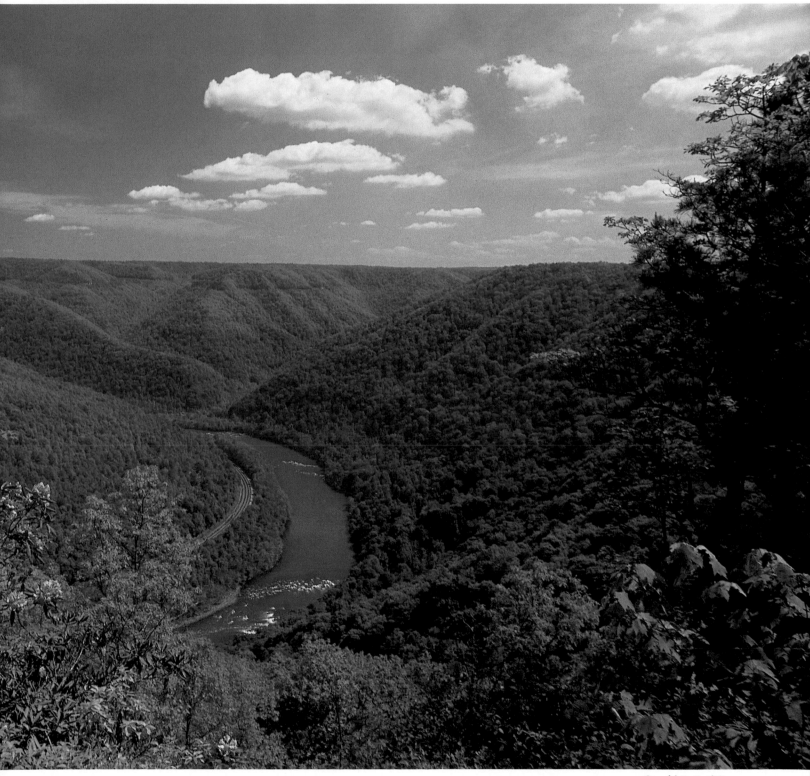

Gerald S. Ratliff

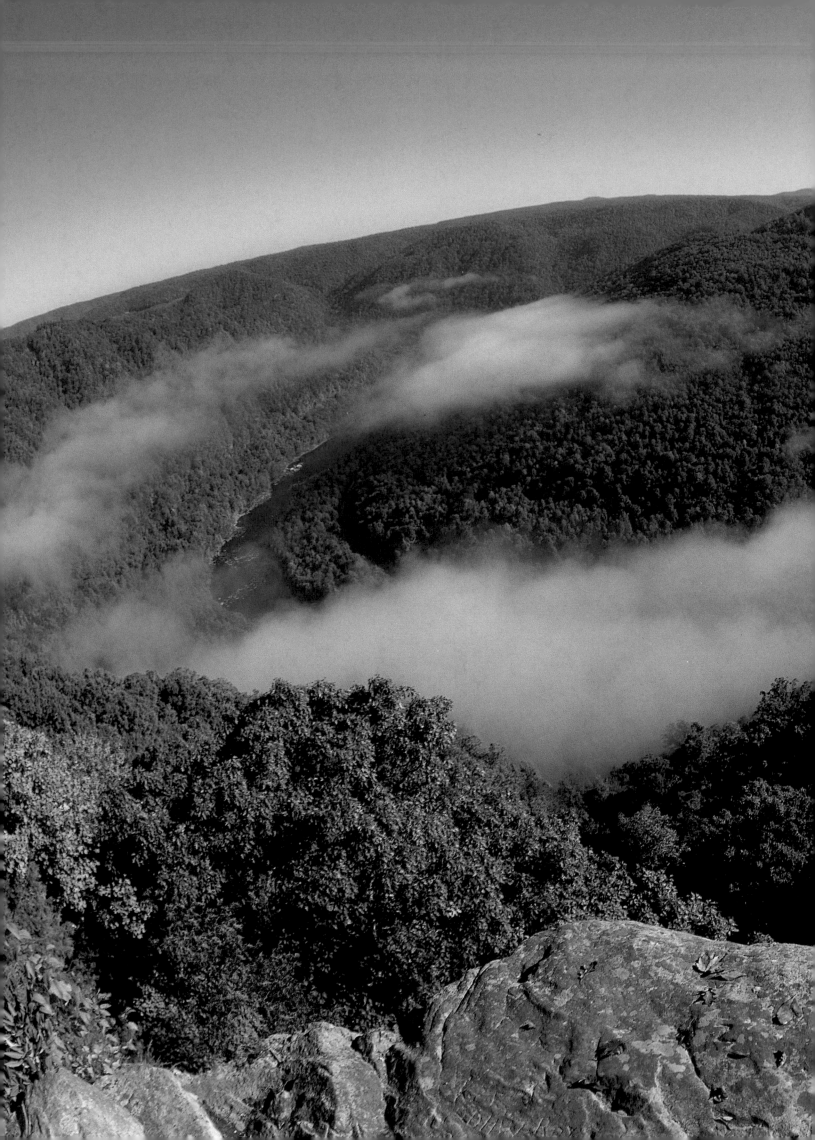

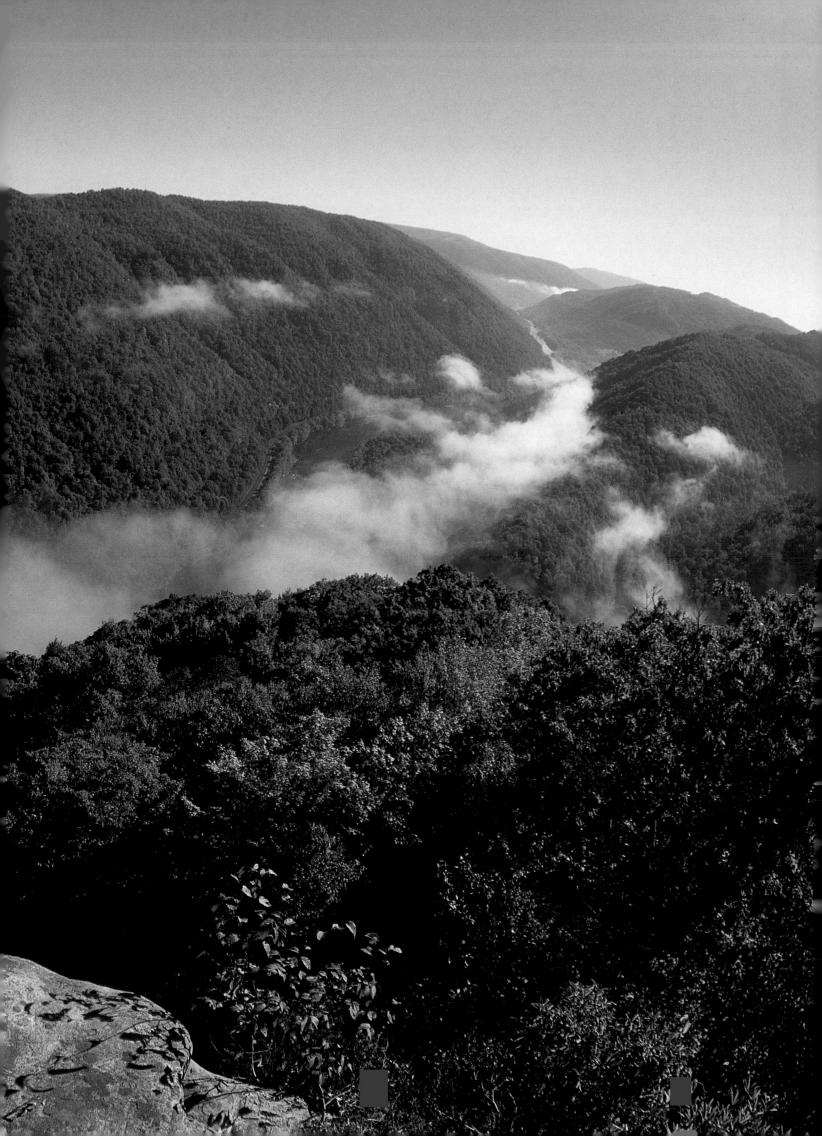

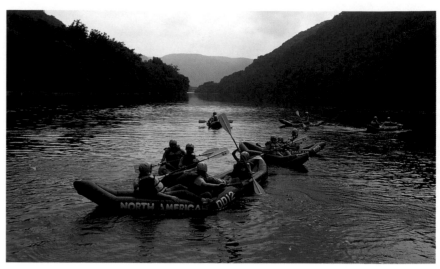

Rubber Duckies begin
their adventure down
the upper stretches of
the New.

Gerald S. Ratliff

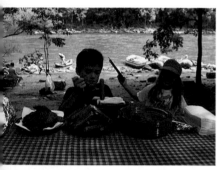

Gerald S. Ratliff

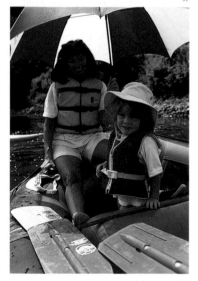

Gerald S. Ratliff

Families enjoy the upper
New on commercial
rafting trips down the
river. .

FLOATING THE UPPER NEW RIVER

From Bluestone Lake to Thurmond, the New is ideally suited for beginning rafters and intermediate whitewater paddlers. Many of the commercial rafting companies offer trips tailored for scout, church and family groups. They use equipment from regular whitewater rafts to inflatable rubber kayaks called rubber duckies. In addition to one-day float trips, camping trips are offered for overnight ventures.

The river is usually divided into three sections, each requiring a day, or part of a day, to float.

From Bluestone Dam to Sandstone Falls, the river flows through a beautiful valley for some eleven miles. The river is quite wide—up to one-half mile—with many fishing camps along the banks. Below Hinton is a long Class 2/3 rapid. After a lengthy stretch of flat water, there is Brooks Falls, which has a formidable 5-foot drop, and requires scouting. It has a Class Rating from 3 to 4. Below Brooks Falls, there are three rapids that can be powerful river ledges and require caution. All boaters should take out well before reaching Sandstone Falls. This is the largest cataract on the New River and is not runable under any conditions.

From Sandstone Falls to McCreery is a 15-mile run through remote country with long stretches of flat water. There is a series of very nice Class 3 rapids which have heavy enough water to swamp an open boat. The mountains narrow down, and a good view of this part of the river can be seen from Grandview Park in the New River National River. Much of the excellent fishing on the New is found here, along with good camping opportunities for overnight trips.

From McCreery to Thurmond is another stretch 15 miles long with heavier rapids than the upper river. Only intermediate paddlers with large water experience should attempt this trip. The river is wide and powerful with beautiful scenery all along the way. Large standing waves are encountered below some of the rapids, plus occasional hydraulics which can hold a boat.

For more detailed information on the river regarding boating information, write Superintendent, New River Gorge National River, P.O. Box 246, Glen Jean, West Virginia 25846. For commercial raft trips, write The Department of Commerce, State Capitol, Charleston, West Virginia 25305. Also, a very excellent book titled "Wildwater West Virginia" by Bob Burrell and Paul Davidson, which serves as a Paddler's Guide to white-water rivers in West Virginia, is available through bookstores. The West Virginia Wildwater Association has organized canoe trips for members throughout this section of the river. This organization was founded in 1965 for the purpose of paddling and conserving the wild and scenic rivers of West Virginia and the surrounding Appalachian area. From the original handful of members, it has grown into a major recreational and conservation organization in the State. Each year, the club takes 40 to 50 science camp students and counselors down the Prince-to-Thurmond section. Persons interested in the WVWA can write P.O. Box 8413, South Charleston, West Virginia 25305.

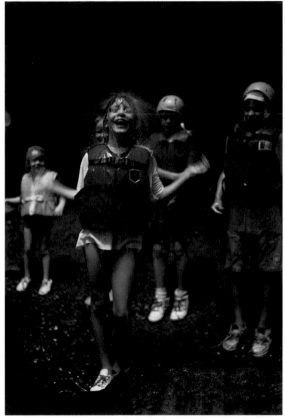

Right; *During the organized rafting trips fun activities abound, such as standing under a waterfall. Below; Joyce Cooper helps lead the annual youth science campers down the river. Forty-four campers and a half dozen camp personnel made the trip in 1990. Each year the West Virginia Wildwater Association helps make this a successful event.*

Gerald S. Ratliff

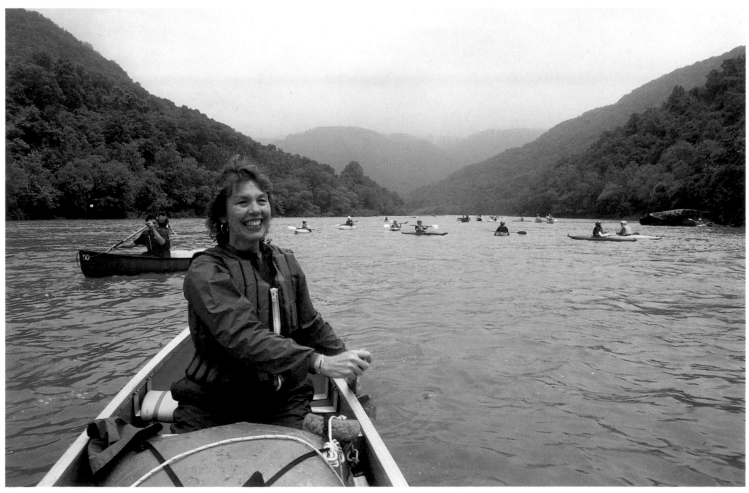

Stephen J. Shaluta Jr.

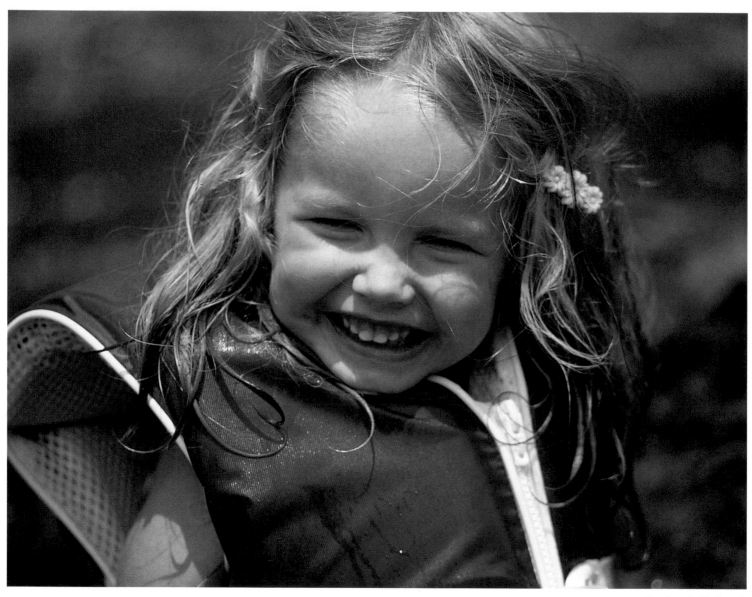

One happy whitewater rafter, three year old Katie Lukacs.

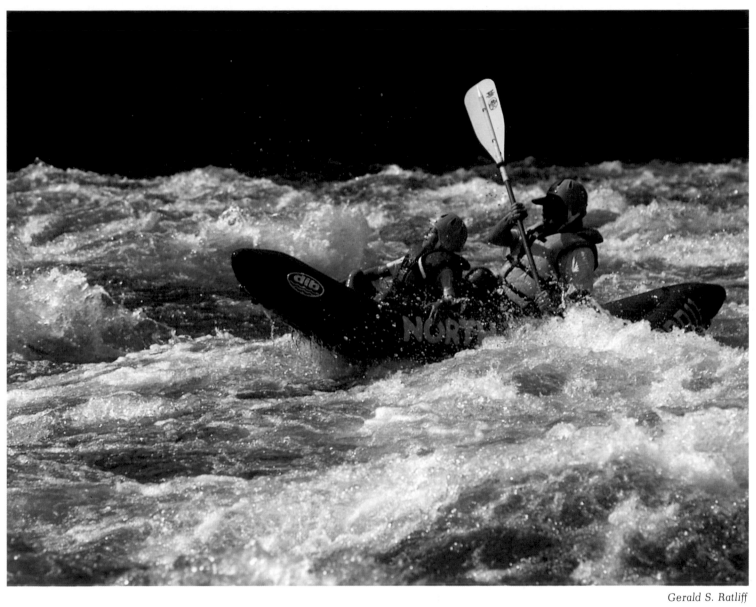

Rubber Duckie rides through a nice rapid on the upper stretch of the New.

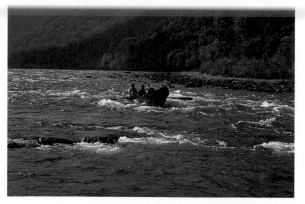

DORIES AND FISHING ON THE NEW RIVER

Drifting down the New River in a dory on a warm summer day, bait casting behind an eddy after running a large rapid, watching the bronze back of a trophy-size smallmouth bass arch through the air before hitting a surface plug—it just doesn't get any better than this.

There are just such trips on the New available from a company called New River Dories. The dory is a flat-bottomed rowboat with a sharp prow, flaring sides and flat triangular stern. These boats, also called Mackenzie drift boats, were designed to withstand the roughest fishing waters in Alaska. They usually carry two fishermen, with an expert guide, who is knowledgeable of the river and knows the best eddies and deep pools where record-size fish are caught.

Many species of game fish thrive in the New. There are walleyes that grow to large size, an abundance of catfish, Kentucky spotted bass, hybrid strippers, muskie, crappies, yellow perch and an occasional largemouth bass. Perhaps the best is the smallmouth bass which, pound for pound, is the hardest fighting freshwater fish to challenge an angler. The New River is considered one of the premier smallmouth bass streams in the country. The current State record for a smallmouth bass is a 7.5 pounder measuring 25.5 inches taken in the New.

Those interested in fishing trips and the home of New River Dories outfitter should contact The Department of Natural Resources or The Department of Commerce, both at the West Virginia State Capitol, Charleston, West Virginia 25305.

The Dories are made to negotiate and withstand heavy rapids.

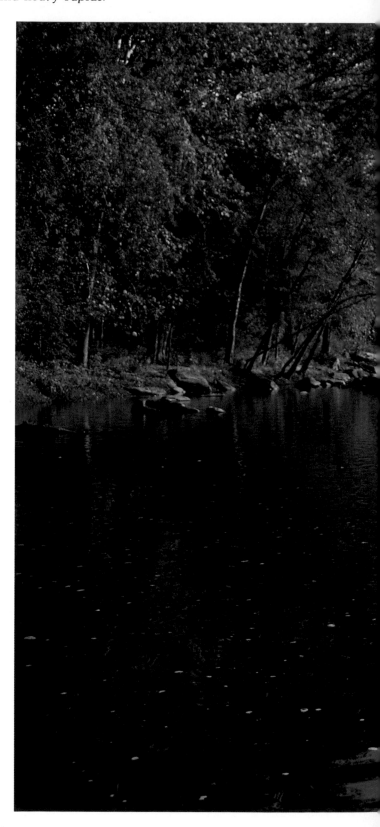

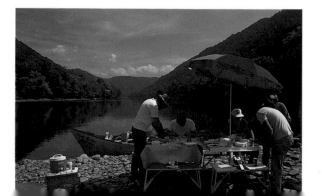

Excellent meals are served on these trips.

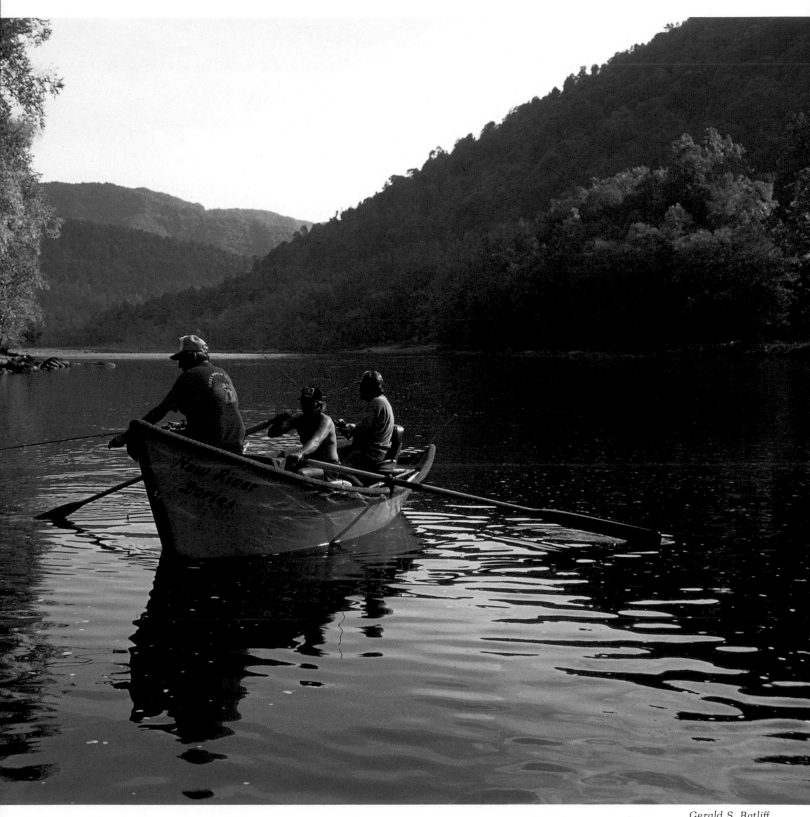

National outdoor magazines have written that this is one of the finest small mouth bass fishing trips available in North America.

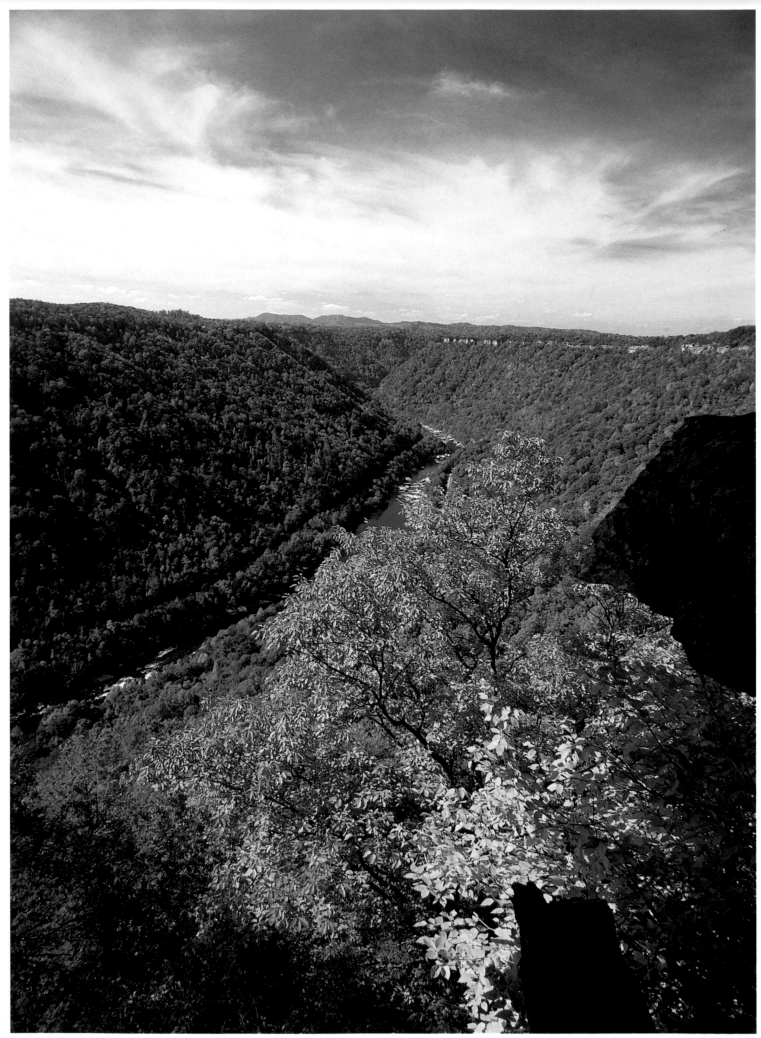

Gerald S. Ratliff

THURMOND
TO HAWKS NEST

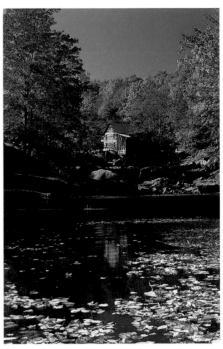

Stephen J. Shaluta Jr.

Old grist mill at Babcock
State Park still grinds
cornmeal. This park
borders the New River
near the old ghost town
of Sewell.

Often called the "Grand Canyon of the East," this spectacular gorge was carved over millions of years and is becoming a premier national park in the east. As the Appalachian land masses rose, the New River sliced through to create this canyon, exposing rocks as old as 330 million years. Geologists estimate each foot of river bottom worn away required thousands of years. As the canyon became deeper and the mountains sides steeper over eons, boulders tumbled into the river, eventually being eroded and washed downstream.

In 1873, the Chesapeake and Ohio completed a railroad through this remote region. Lumbering, coal mining and coke making industries prospered. By 1900, 13 towns existed between Thurmond and Fayette Station. Today, not a single person resides in the area separating these two towns.

From a 23-room mansion built by Colonel Joseph L. Beury, who shipped out the first New River coal, to the many saloons with such names as Black Hawk, Bloody Bucket, Dime a Dozen and Stagger Lee, the region became a legacy of fascinating stories of a boom and bust time. Even Henry Ford owned a mine at Nuttallburg, which he visited on occasion, while the local boys in town owned Model-T Fords that were adapted to run on the railroad tracks. Come Saturday night these lads had a grand time racing up and down the tracks in their Model-Ts.

Jon Dragan, in 1968, started the first commercial whitewater rafting trips down the river. This was the beginning of a major new industry. Presently, over 20 companies operate whitewater trips. Rock climbing, also, has grown in popularity along the cliffs in the gorge.

With the area under the protection of the National Park Service, this magnificent canyon is now preserved to be enjoyed for its recreation and beauty in the years to come.

View of the Gorge
from Beauty Mountain.

Right; *Walls of buildings are reminders of the past.* Below; *Drawing coke from ovens in the Gorge. Date unknown.* Beneath; *Abandoned coal mine tipple at Nuttallburg.*

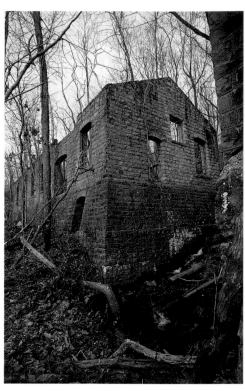

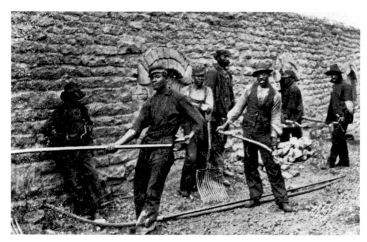

Courtesy; *New River Gorge National River*

Gerald S. Ratliff

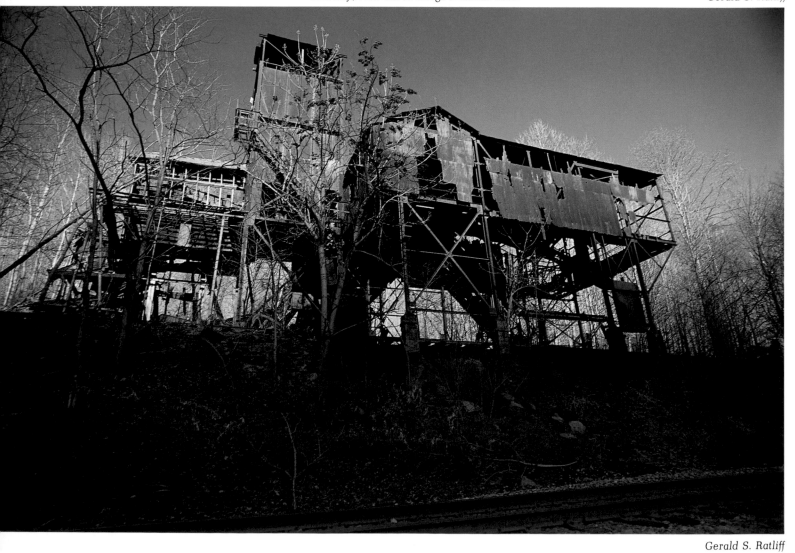

Gerald S. Ratliff

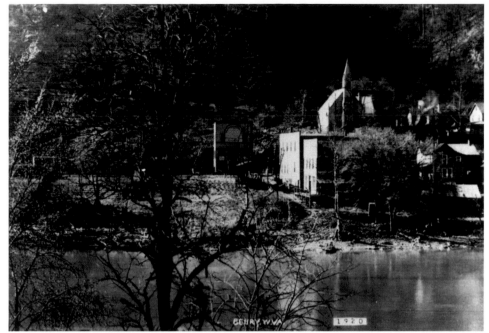

Left; *The town of Beury in the Gorge in 1920. Below; An old chimney and fireplace once gave warmth to inhabitants living in the region.*

Courtesy; New River Gorge National River

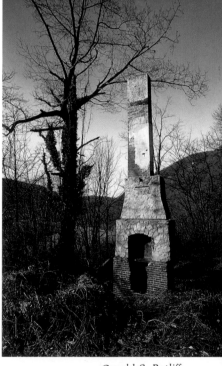

Gerald S. Ratliff

Overleaf: *Old mining tipple at Nuttallburg. Inserts; Exterior of the Beury Mansion. Interior of the Beury Mansion with wedding presents for Daisy Beury's wedding to Thomas Nickel. Nurses at the McKendree Hospital and "Ophia Godbey Nurses Home" about 1928. Coke ovens at Sewell.*

YESTERDAY IN THE GORGE

A train ride down the Gorge 80 years ago would have presented a much different scene than it does now. That was a time when boom coal mining towns hugged the sides of the mountains. Names like Nuttalburg, Kaymoor, Caperton, Swell, Red Ash, Fire Creek, Beury and Thurmond marked the map. With these towns came European immigrants to mine the coal, lay track and timber the surrounding mountains. Coal barons became wealthy and built fine mansions in the Gorge. An ominous haze of sulphurous gases from steam locomotives and mile-long coke ovens prevailed during these times.

Many saloons popped up, giving an air of lawlessness to the territory. Many an unfortunate individual who lost an argument over a woman, booze, dice and cards wound up in the New River. In the Gorge there was another way of life. Families attended church and went to socials. Schools helped with reading and writing and arithmetic; a large miners' hospital trained nurses.

As the coal seams were mined out, the towns became deserted. By 1950, the coal era had ended, and the Gorge fell into silence with only the roar of the river and an occasional train passing by. The old wooden buildings deteriorated under the warm summer rains, with roofs caving in under the weight of snow, and trees growing between the old walls of foundations. Today, these ghost towns are mostly stone foundations, rusting tipples, and overgrown railroad tracks; a legacy up and down the Gorge of a once thriving way of late 19th- and early 20th-century life.

Black and White Photos Next Page. Courtesy; New River Gorge National River.

Overleaf; Gerald S. Ratliff

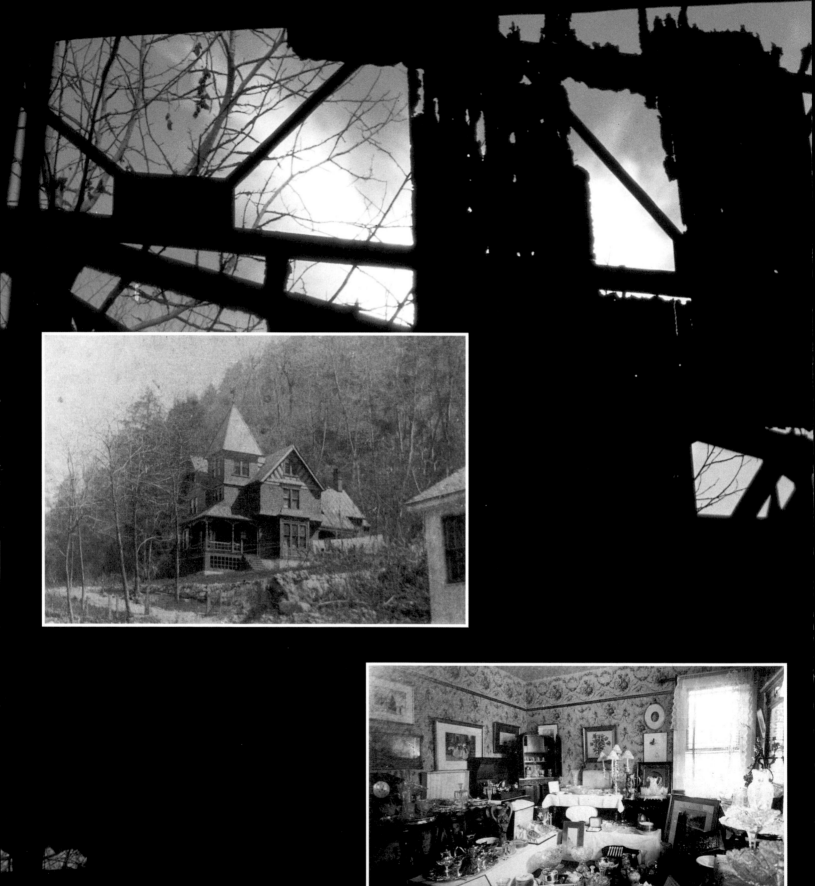

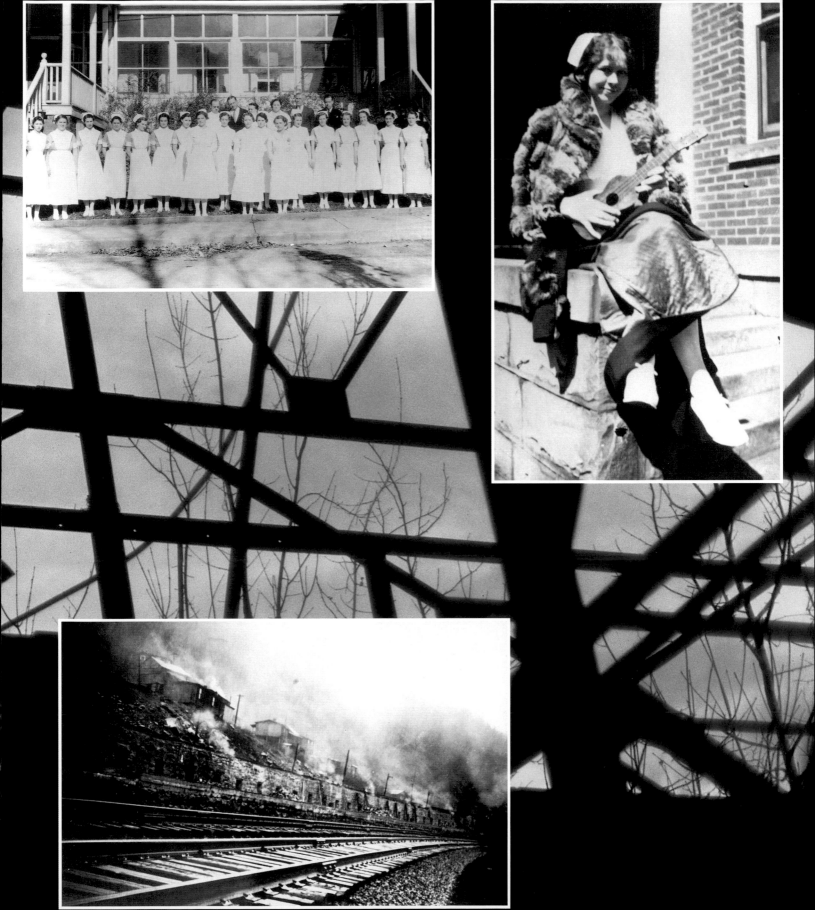

NEW RIVER GORGE NATIONAL RIVER

For many years, the United States Congress has been safeguarding strategic areas of the nation from commercial exploitation. This is done by designating land as national parks and portions of streams as national rivers. Some criteria used in evaluating an area for protection are historical, natural and scenic beauty, endangered wildlife habitat and other unique features.

During 1959, studies were initiated which culminated in national status for the New River Gorge in 1978. Congress authorized the purchase of 60,000 acres, and the Park Service now owns 35,000. The State of West Virginia recently ceded the 900-acre Grandview State Park to the Park Service for inclusion in the federal facility.

The Park Service recognizes West Virginia as an important tourist mecca and has an active program developing public facilities involving the Gorge. Some of the projects expected to be in progress during 1991 are: Canyon Rim Visitor Center, Glen Jean Bank Building restoration, Sandstone Falls boardwalk and bridge, and reconditioning historic buildings in Thurmond. When these and other projects in the planning stage are completed, the Gorge system will be one of the finest national park areas in the National Park System.

There are several hiking trails now available and more in the planning stage. Of special interest will be the Mary Draper Ingles Trail through the 55-mile length of the park. This trail will eventually run from Virginia to Ohio, following the route Mary Ingles and her companion covered during their escape from the Shawnee Indians.

Theatre West Virginia will continue to present dramas in the Grandview amphitheater. There will be a 90-seat capacity theatre in the new Canyon Rim Visitor Center to be used primarily for slide shows of public use sites in West Virginia.

Whitewater sports will continue to be a major drawing card for the region. Recent Congressional action creating the Gauley River National Recreation Area and the Bluestone National Scenic River gives the Park Service over 100 miles of whitewater rapids to administer.

Expectations are high for the future of the New River Gorge, becoming one of America's premier national parks.

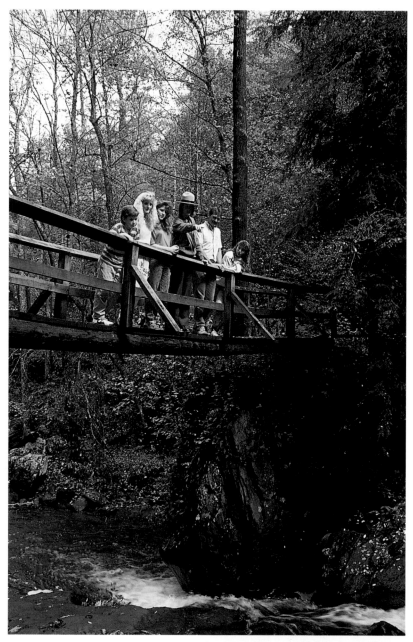

Stephen J. Shaluta Jr.

Top; *Park Ranger Lizzie Watts points out attractions along the Kaymoor Trail.* Right; *Teka K. Lamade and John Hartman bike along the Ingles Trail between Thurmond and Minden.*

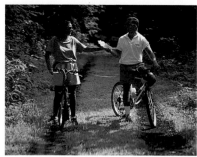

Stephen J. Shaluta Jr.

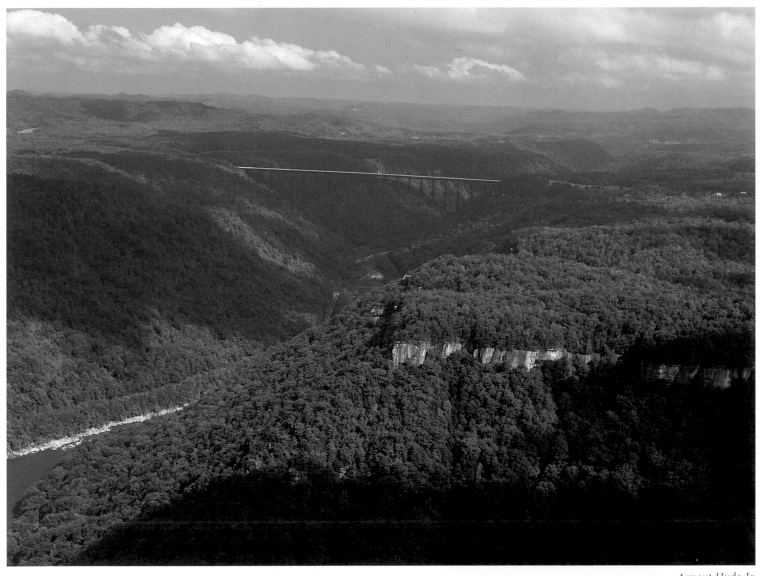

Arnout Hyde Jr.

Top; A band of 325-million-year-old quartzose conglomerate sandstone (Nuttall Sandstone), which has attracted climbers since 1974, parallels the canyon walls below the rim. These cliffs are made up of sedimentary rock and are resistant to weathering due to a high mixture of quartz found in the sandstone. Right; Andy Dappen climbs Junkyard Wall in the New River Gorge. Overleaf; Climber Rick Mix rappeling Photo Finish Route on Mountain in the Gorge.

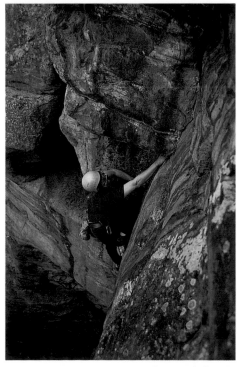

Stephen J. Shaluta Jr.

Overleaf; Stephen J. Shaluta Jr.

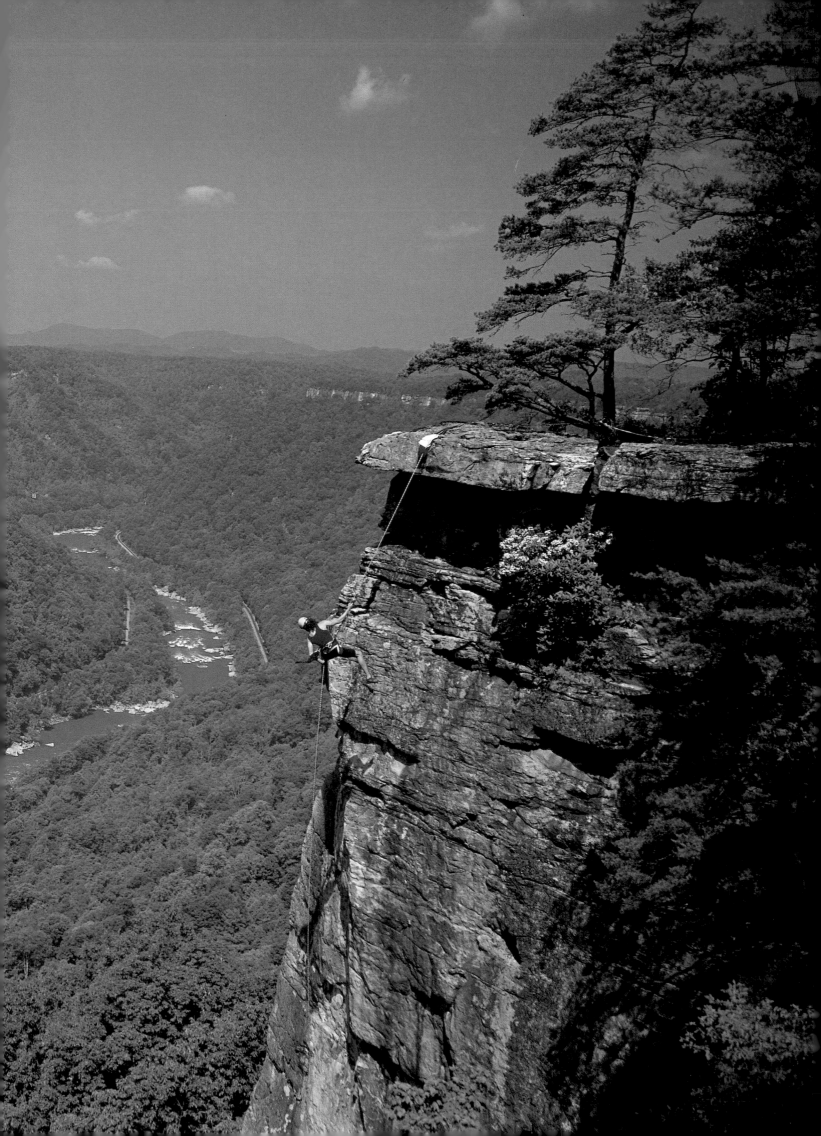

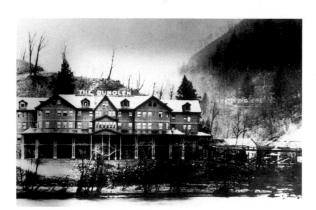

Courtesy; New River Gorge National River

The Dunglen Hotel.

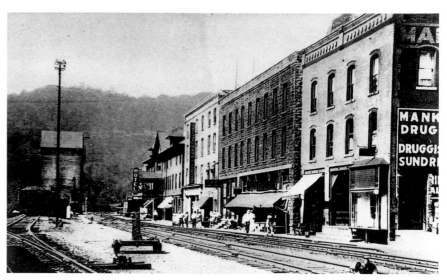

Courtesy; New River Gorge National River

Thurmond in its heyday.

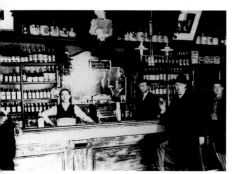

Courtesy; New River Gorge
National River

Top; *Typical saloon of the area. Opposite Page; Thurmond seen through the broken windows of the railroad repair shop across the tracks.*

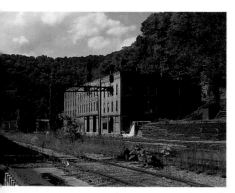

Arnout Hyde Jr.

Thurmond today.

THURMOND

There was a town in the gorge whose infamous reputation prompted Rev. Shirley Donnelly to write, "The only difference between Hell and Thurmond was in that a river ran through Thurmond."

In the late 1800s, tracts of land on opposite sides of the New River caused a dispute over varying philosophies on how a town should operate. Captain William D. Thurmond owned land on the east side, while Thomas G. McKell had land along Dunlop Creek, which bordered the river on the opposite side. In addition, McKell had a ten-mile stretch of railroad along Dunlop Creek which crossed the river at Thurmond. Dispute arose over moral issues such as, could a hotel serve drinks at a bar. By 1906, on Thurmond's side of town, there were several theaters, a barbershop, bank, drugstore and other businesses. On the other side, in 1901, Thomas G. McKell built the famous Dunglen Hotel that started a wide open area, not unlike the old Wild West. This hotel had a hundred rooms, four and one half stories, a wide veranda and all the lavish trappings of the day. When the hotel opened, the Cincinnati Symphony Orchestra came to perform for a grand opening dance, in which 100 couples—many being prominent West Virginians—danced the night away.

The Dunglen gained a national reputation during the next 13 or so years, with a bar that never closed and a gambling room which had the longest known continuous poker game of 14 years. All of life's pleasures of the day could be found there. It was a time when coal operators, newly rich, threw lavish parties at the Dunglen. The town's famed reputation attracted gamblers, businessmen and politicians from Washington, D.C., all coming by train. In fact, the only way in and out of Thurmond was by train and as many as twenty trains stopped there daily. More freight was handled at Thurmond than in a city the size of Cincinnati. Whiskey, women and cards arrived daily by train.

The lawman Harrison Ash, a police officer in the town, had seven notches carved in the handle of his pistol and the respect of the evildoers around town. It is said he fined a dead man, pulled from the New River, $80, a watch, and a pistol—just what the poor fellow had on him. The charge: carrying a concealed weapon. It was not uncommon to find a body floating downstream in the New after a wild night in Thurmond.

Prohibition, roads into the town, a bank failure and a bad name slowly closed the wild side of Thurmond. In 1930, the Dunglen Hotel burned. However, the town remained an important railroad center in the gorge. It also had another side seldom written about, but in a recent article in WONDERFUL WEST VIRGINIA magazine, Larry S. Richmond wrote about the good things of Thurmond he remembered as a child. He described valentine parties, church picnics, fishing and swimming in the New, and the best was knowing the many fine people who lived there.

Much of Thurmond remains a ghost town, and it was the setting for the recent movie "Matewan," a story of the mine wars in West Virginia.

Arnout Hyde Jr

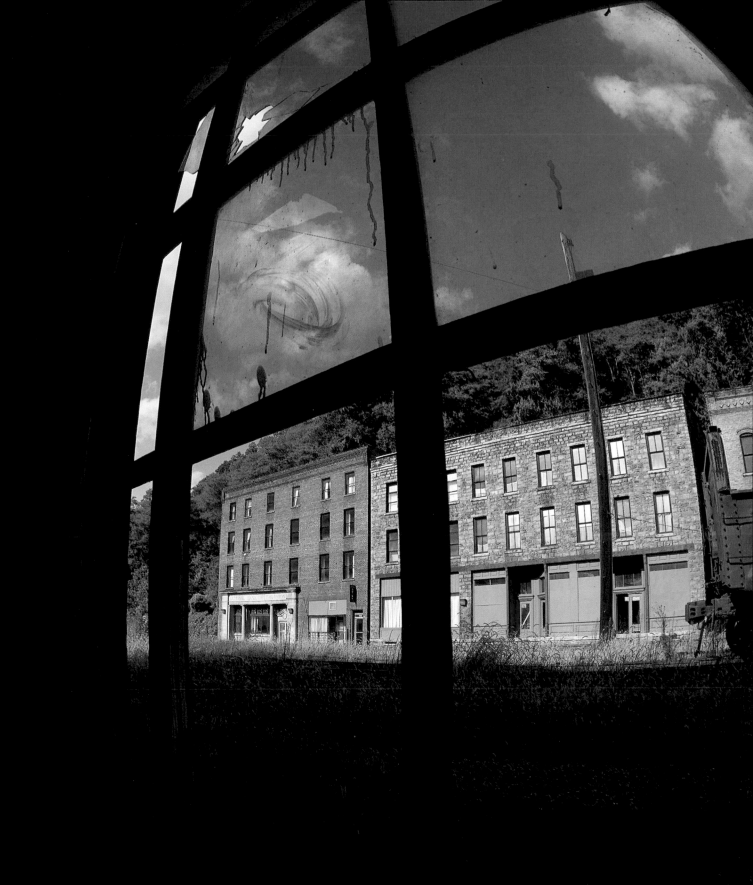

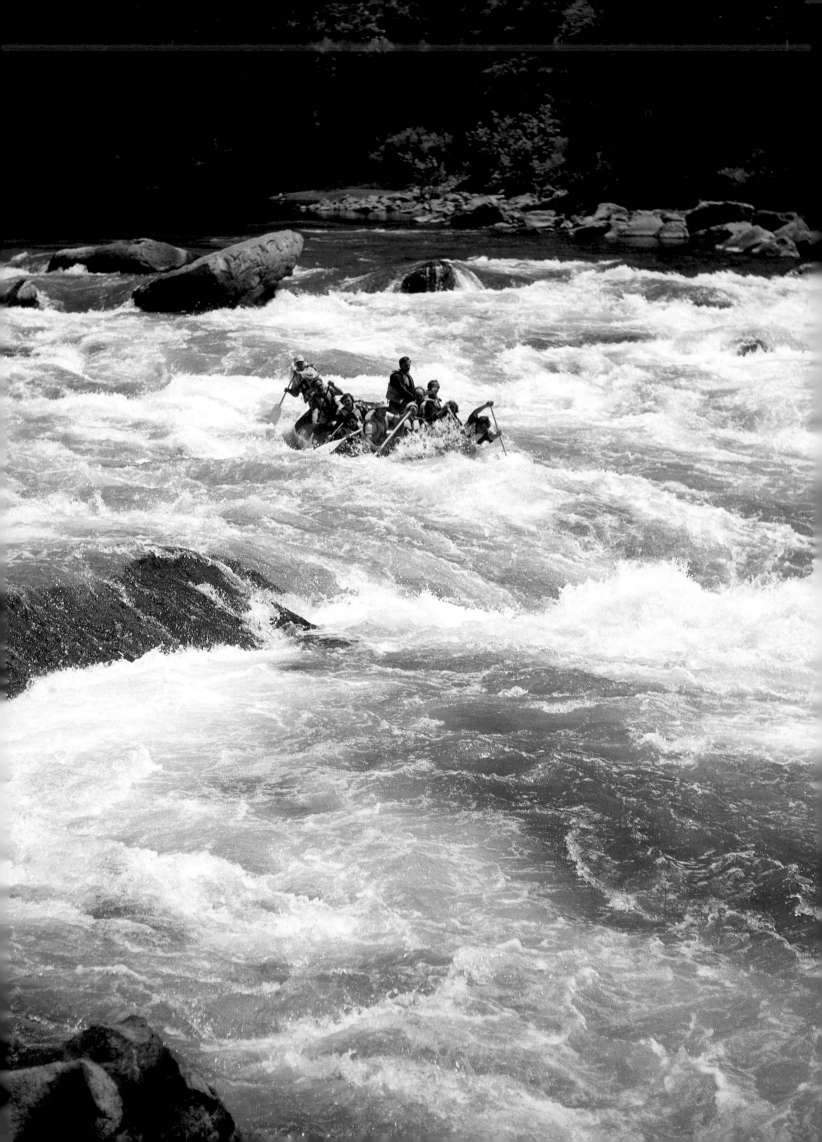

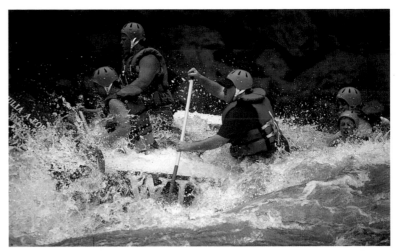

An exhilarating ride through whitewater.

WHITEWATER RECREATION IN THE GORGE

Hydraulics is the scientific term applied to the laws of liquids. Hydraulically speaking, water flowing over boulders and ledges in a stream bed creates something wonderful—whitewater, which the New River is famous for. Capitalizing on these numerous rapids, especially in the gorge, an enterprising whitewater rafting business has sprung up in the last 20 years.

Two reasons the Lower New has become recognized as one of the best whitewater rivers in the country are the varying complexity of the rapids, and that the river is runable year-round. This is West Virginia's biggest whitewater river. It is almost as though this portion of the river was planned for commercial rafting in that the trip takes a day, with the first rapids being moderately difficult—ideal for learning paddling techniques early on. As the river enters the gorge with rugged mountains on either side, the river is restricted, and the gradient becomes steeper, creating numerous difficult rapids. By mid-trip, rafters are in the big stuff, and everyone is wet, yelling and paddling like mad.

The American Whitewater Affiliation rates rapids from 1 to 6, 1 being the easiest with small riffles; and 6 on the other end of the scale, defined as the utmost in difficulty and a risk to life. This stretch of river has class 5 rapids, perfect for the adventurous.

Each of the major rapids is named, starting with Surprise, Upper Railroad, Lower Railroad, Upper Keeney, Middle Keeney, Lower Keeney, Double Z, Greyhound Bus Stopper, Upper and Lower Kaymoor, Miller's Folly and Fayette Station Rapid.

Unique to the whitewater fraternity, there are colorful vocabulary terms describing different river situations. ROCK GARDEN—exposed and partly exposed rocks that require expertise in maneuvering. HYDRAULIC—a condition where water moves over a ledge, creating a downward action of water, which might hold a boat in one place. CURLER—a wave that falls back on itself. HAYSTACK—a high standing wave. SURFING WAVE—a wide wave whereby a boater can travel back and forth, while facing upriver. KEEPER—a dangerous hydraulic that will hold a boat regardless of how hard one paddles. POOL—flat water. EDDY—a reverse flow of water, usually at the end and to one side of a rapid. A good place to rest.

Once on the river, the guide in charge of the raft will shout directions over the roar of the rapids: paddle right, now left, hold up, back paddle, now paddle like hell to clear that rock. Between rapids, splash battles often break out between rafts. Excellent lunches are served along the riverbank. During the trip, the guides explain the history of the gorge, noting especially the early thriving coal mining communities, now ghost towns. Also throughout the trip, private boats, primarily kayaks, can be seen bobbing and twisting through the rapids.

The rafting industry is regulated by the West Virginia Department of Natural Resources, which requires all guides to be skilled river people trained in techniques of river safety, first aid and CPR. Information and addresses on whitewater companies operating on the New River can be obtained by writing the West Virginia Department of Commerce, State Capitol, Charleston, West Virginia 25305.

Rafters plow through rapids on the lower stretch of the New.

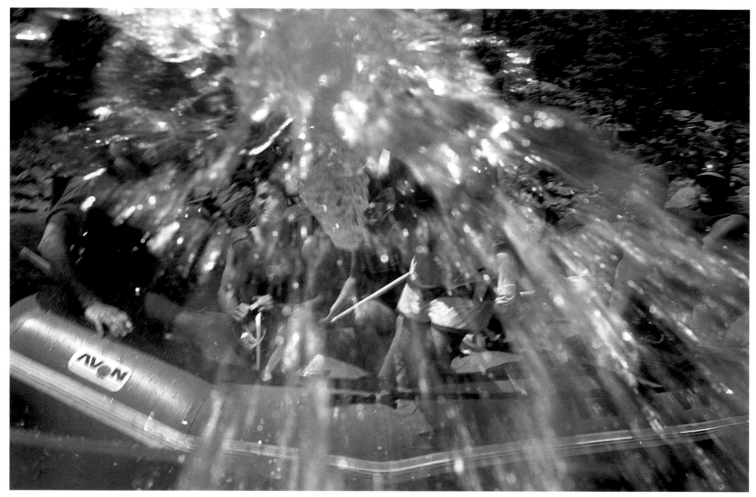

Arnout Hyde Jr.

Often splash battles break out between rival rafts.

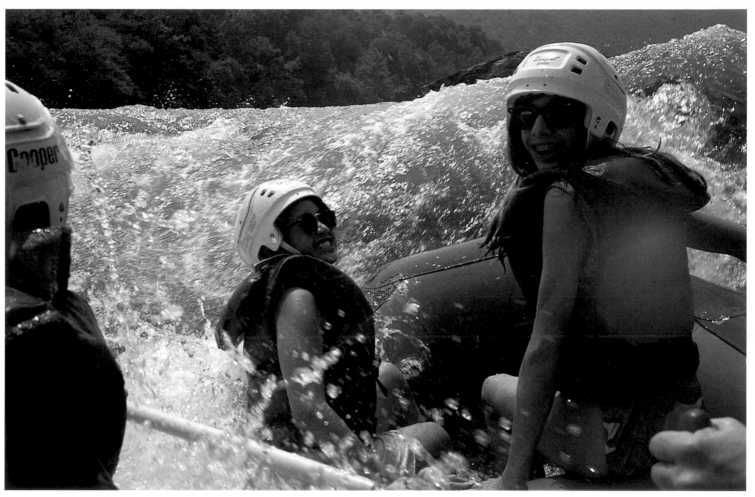

Two cool rafters, Lucia and Karen, pause with a grin, before hitting a wall of water.

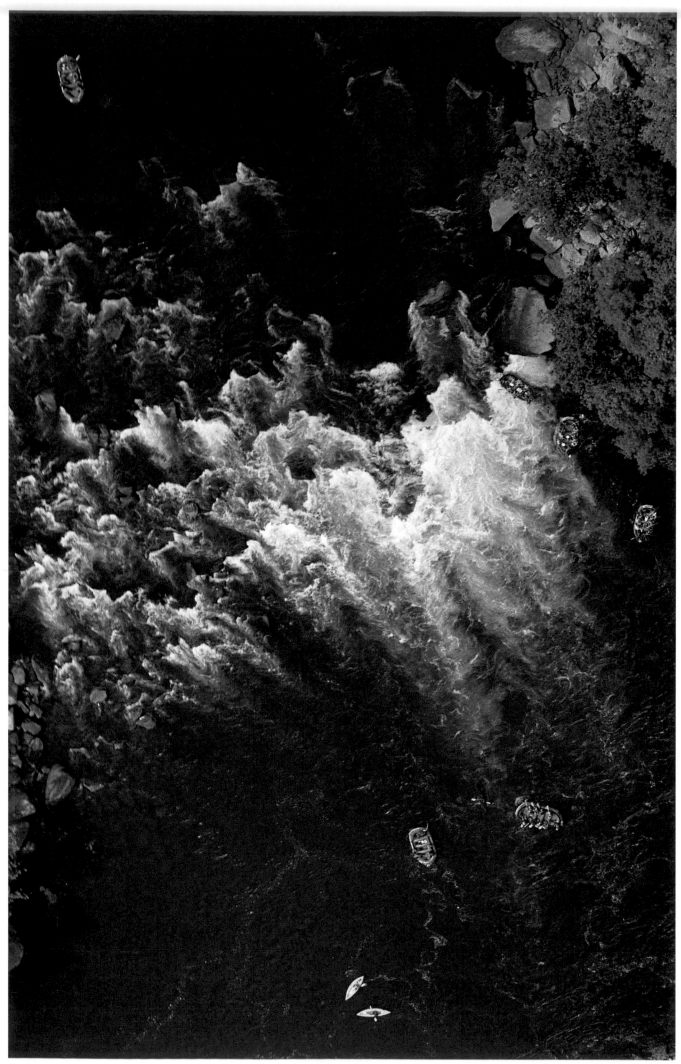

Arnout Hyde Jr.

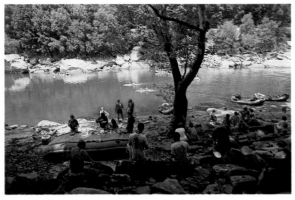

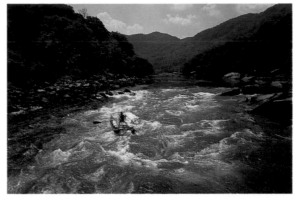

Arnout Hyde Jr.   *Arnout Hyde Jr.*

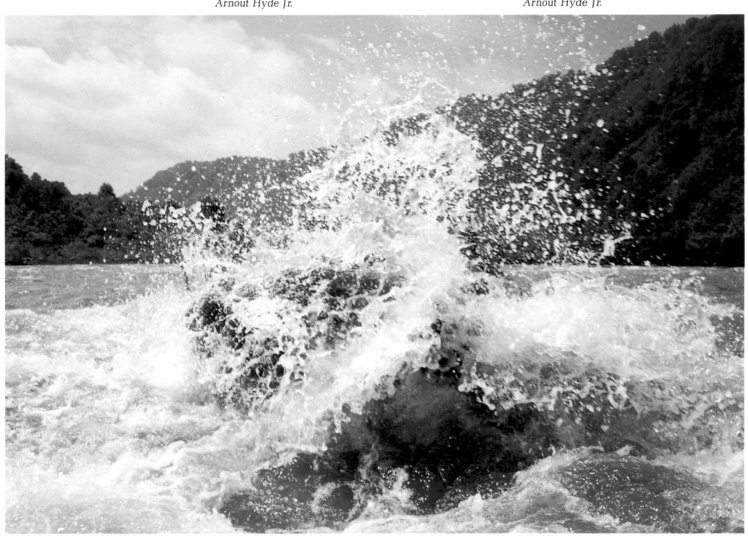

Arnout Hyde Jr.

Top Left; *The rafting companies offer excellent lunches, and often a raft is turned over for a table.* Top Right; *Not all vessels coming down the river are rafts and kayaks.* Above; *A raft hits a standing wave, drenching rafters.* Opposite Page; *Aerial view of rafts and kayaks as they negotiate Lower Railroad rapids.*

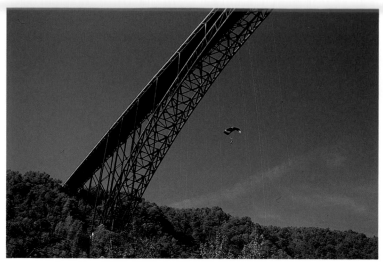

Gerald S Ratliff

Base jumper takes the plunge.

NEW RIVER GORGE BRIDGE—BRIDGE DAY

Appalachian Corridor L connects Interstate 79 and the West Virginia Turnpike, crossing the New River near Fayetteville with the longest single-span arch bridge in the world. This impressive structure is the highest bridge east of the Mississippi River. The bridge towers 875 feet above the New River, with a total span of 3,030 feet. COR-TEN steel, which never needs painting, was used. The steel oxidizes, forming a protective coating of rust, which creates a russet color. This color is aesthetically complementary to the surrounding environment, matching some of the autumn colors. The bridge was completed October 22, 1977, at a cost of 37 million dollars.

Each year on the third Saturday of October, the Fayette County Chamber of Commerce hosts Bridge Day. This is the one time of the year spectators can legally walk across the bridge to view the Gorge below. Also, an all-West Virginia festival is held, featuring crafts and home-cooked food for sale. Musicians and hot air balloons entertain visitors. One of the highlights of Bridge Day is the base jumpers. Six hundred or more jump from the bridge railing, experiencing the thrill of their parachutes opening between the bridge and the river below, all occurring in about 8 seconds.

The new 8,700-square-foot Canyon Rim Visitor Center at New River Gorge National River is in this vicinity.

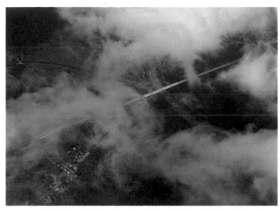

Left; *Aerial view through the clouds of the New River Gorge Bridge.* Bottom; *New River Gorge Bridge with the old bridge at Fayette Station.*

Arnout Hyde Jr.

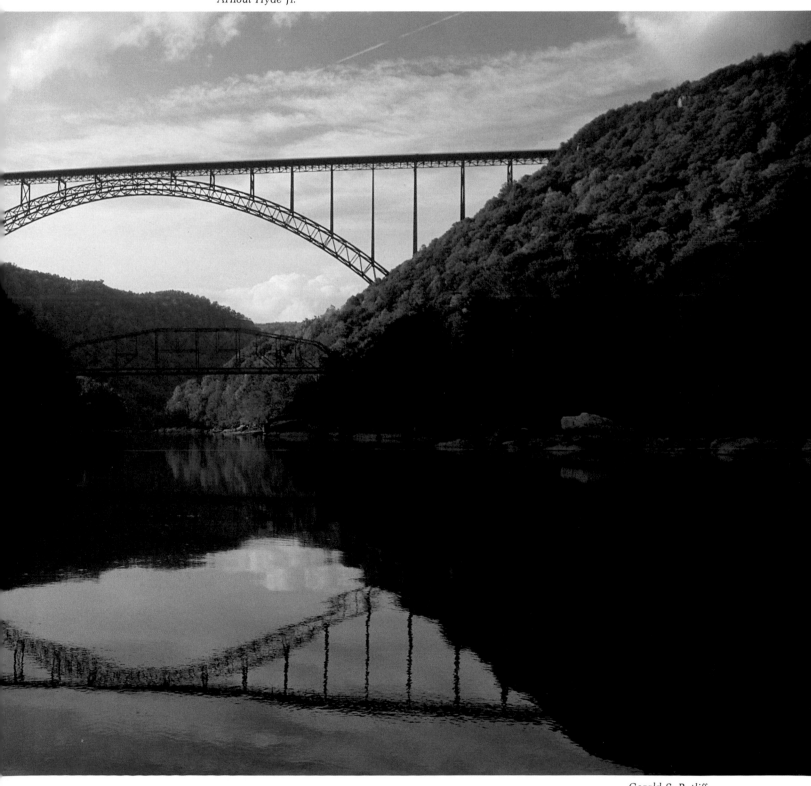

Gerald S. Ratliff

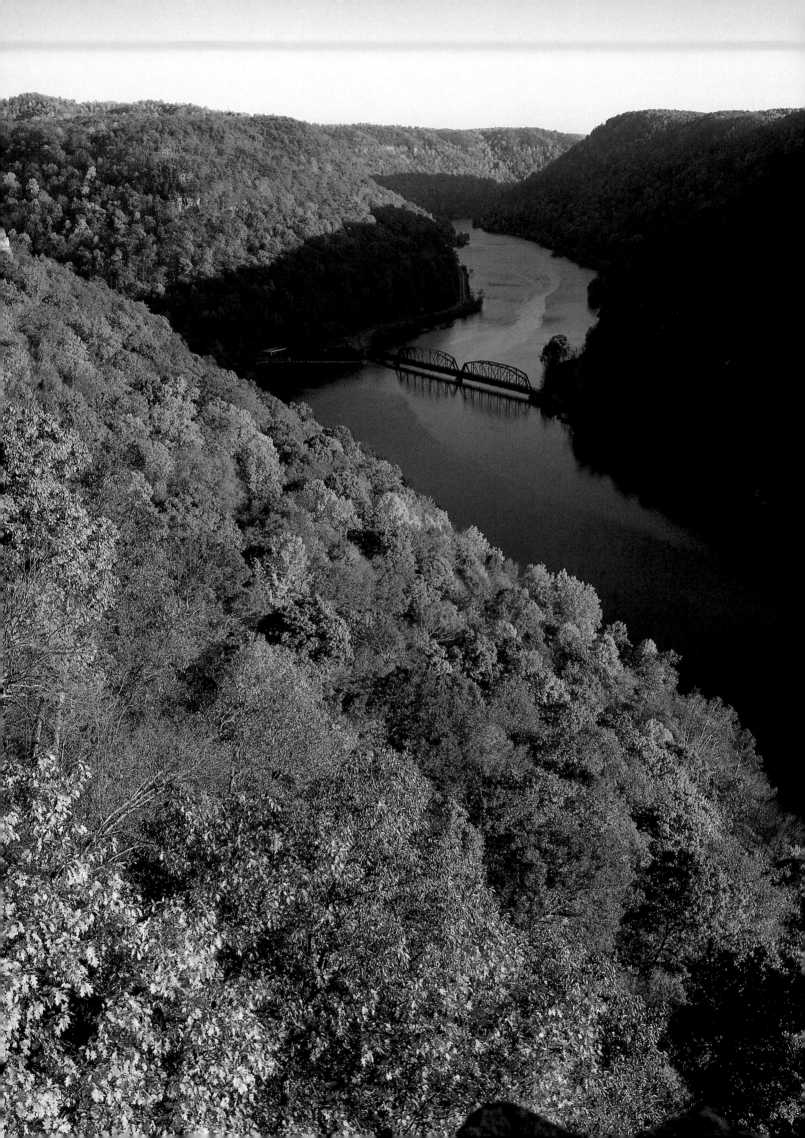

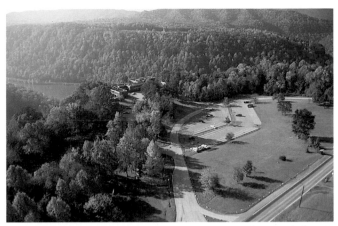

Stephen J. Shaluta Jr.

Aerial view of the lodge at Hawks Nest State Park.

HAWKS NEST
TO GAULEY BRIDGE

An Indian legend lives among the cliffs at Hawks Nest. Little Fawn, a young Cherokee maiden, and Running Deer, a Shawnee brave, wishing to become lovers, were denied this union by their respective families. Consequently, they jumped to their deaths from these cliffs. The rock from which they jumped became known as Lovers Leap Rock.

In the 1930's, the National Park Service, with help from the Civilian Conservation Corps, built picnic shelters, a souvenir shop, museum and overlooks along highway Route 60 on Gauley Mountain, thus opening the way for the forthcoming Hawks Nest State Park. A modern lodge was added in 1967, followed by an aerial tram descending to the river. Private industrial interests constructed a 40-foot dam on the river below the park. The dam diverts the entire normal flow of the river through a 3.2-mile tunnel, drilled through the mountain for hydroelectric generation. The water is returned to the river through a hydroelectric plant. The electric power serves a metallurgical plant at Alloy.

Tunnel construction has become infamous because of the high employee death rate. A 5.3-mile stretch of river bed below the dam is called "Drys" by river enthusiasts, since there is little flow during much of the year. When the water level gets higher than normal and exceeds 3.5 feet at Hinton and 4 feet at Fayette Station, excess water is discharged from the dam, filling the boulder-strewn, dry stream bed with surging masses of white water.

The New River finishes its journey at Gauley Bridge, a quaint town surrounded by beautiful rugged mountains. It is here the New River joins the Gauley River, forming the Kanawha River.

View of New River from Hawks Nest State Park.

Arnout Hyde Jr.

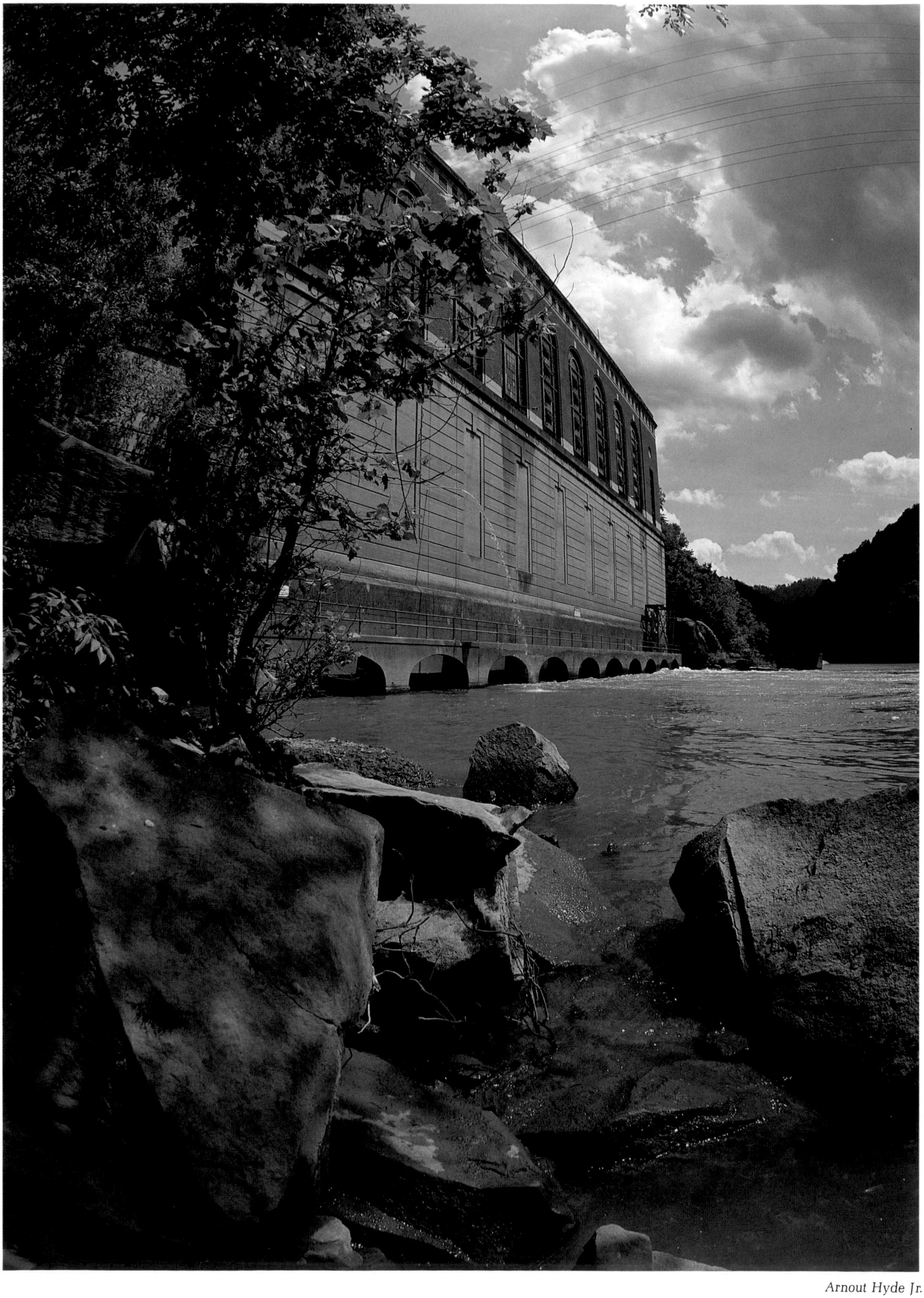

Arnout Hyde Jr.

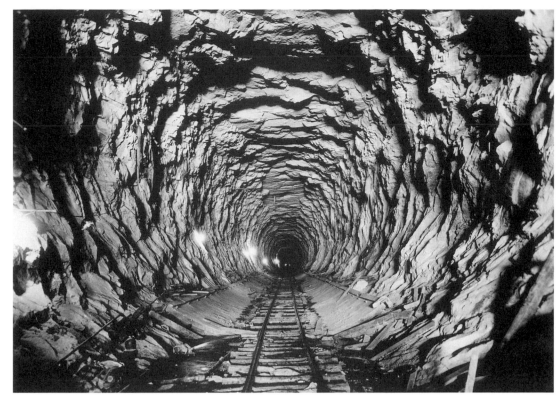

WV Dept. of Culture and History

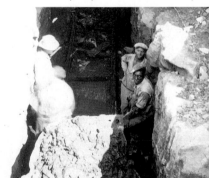

WV Dept. of Culture and History

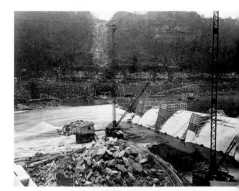

WV Dept. of Culture and History

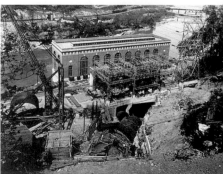

WV Dept. of Culture and History

HAWKS NEST TUNNEL

Construction of the Hawks Nest Tunnel hydroelectric facility in 1934 was remarkable in a number of respects. The engineering overall was superb, but industrial hygiene and safety were catastrophic, and a private entity controlling a public waterway was unusual.

The sole objective of the project was to generate electricity to serve a metallurgical plant to be built at Alloy, West Virginia.

A dam was built on the New River near Hawks Nest, and its entire normal flow was diverted through a 3.2-mile long tunnel drilled through Gauley Mountain to a power plant near Gauley Bridge.

Initial design of the tunnel indicated it was to be 32 feet in diameter; however, after the first 800–1,000 feet in length, it was enlarged to 46 feet. From this point, drilling was through high-grade silicon ore which was a valuable raw material for the future alloy metallurgical plant. The initial and terminal portions through shale and coal seams were concrete-reinforced while the section through solid silica rock supported itself.

It is a tribute to the quality of engineering skill that the overall project—from dam through tunnel to the power generating facilities—is functioning effectively 58 years later.

From a labor point of view, the picture was and is dismal. It has been called "America's worst industrial accident." Many conflicting records and data used during numerous subsequent lawsuits have not survived; therefore, actual death toll estimates vary widely. They range from 100 to 1,500, with the most accepted figure being 500 deaths. In terms of today's more enlightened industrial hygiene climate, it is hard to understand that such a thing could have happened just a short time ago.

The number of typical injuries usually connected with this type of construction project was not unusual. The real problem was silicon dust which caused acute silicosis, often a fatal lung disease. Industrial medicine should have been aware of silicosis since the experience of African gold mines had been well documented.

The "great depression" was in full force and jobs were very scarce. An estimated 5,000 laborers were employed during two years; most were itinerant Negroes from southern states. Many were buried without careful records being kept.

There were 336 grievance lawsuits filed, from which the most successful received only several hundred dollars. A congressional hearing following the tragedy did little to help Hawks Nest sufferers, but labor did gain subsequent legislation controlling working conditions.

Overleaf; *Cathedral Falls on Route 60, the last major tributary to the New.*

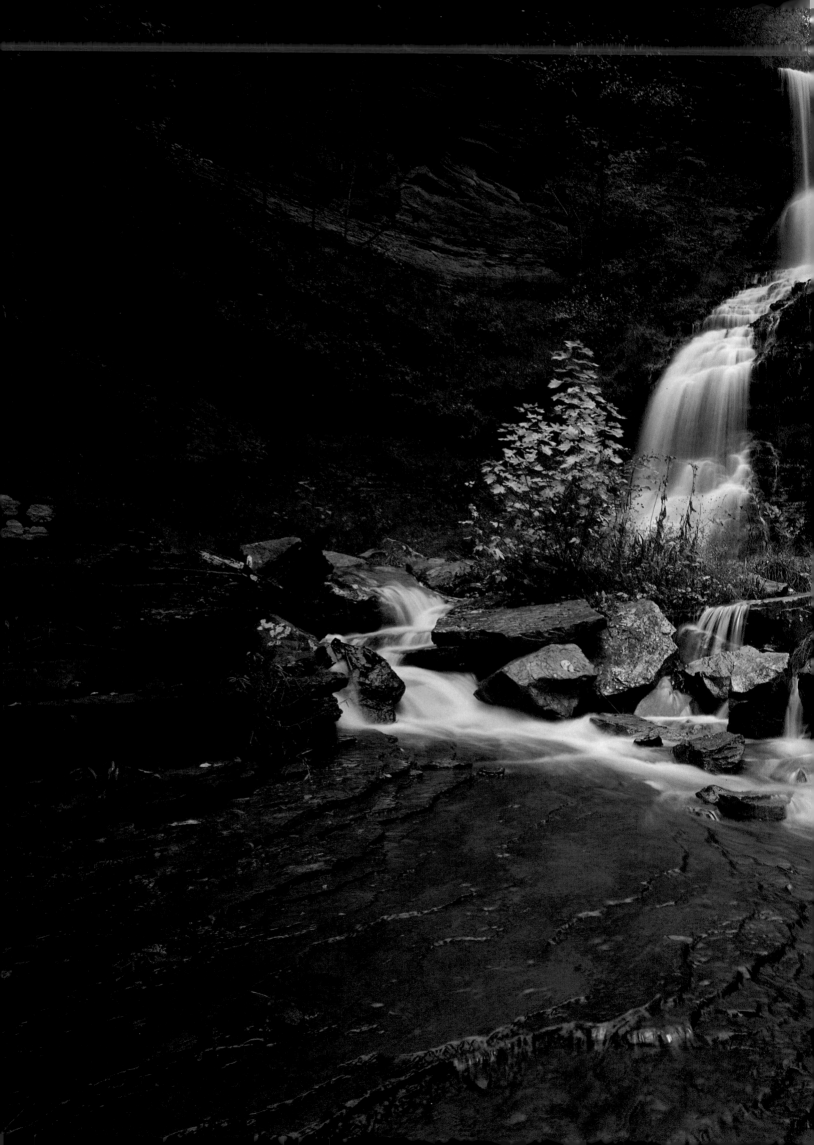

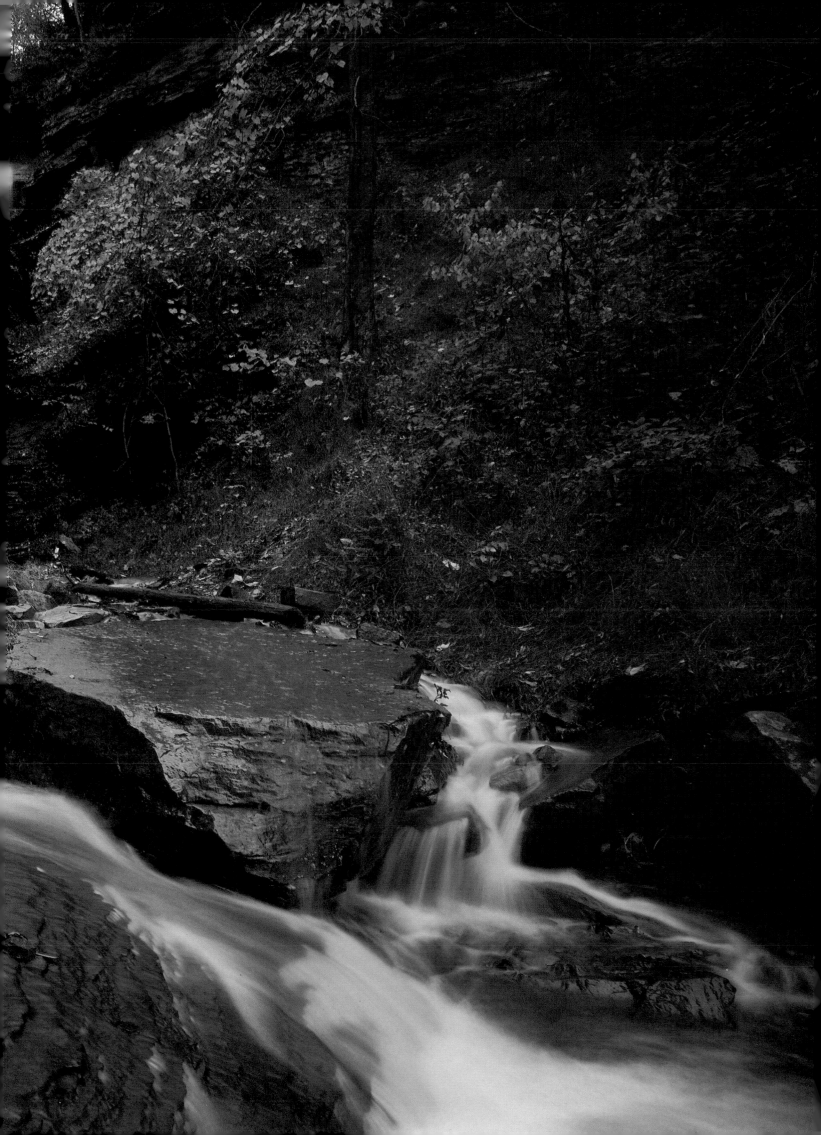

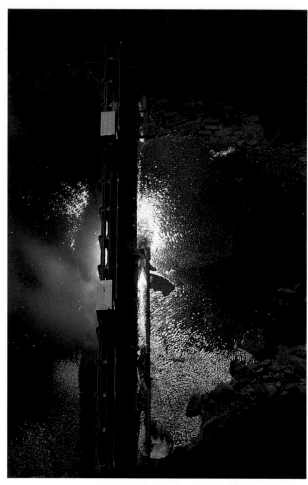

Arnout Hyde Jr.

Left; *Aerial view of Hawks Nest Dam. Opposite Page; River below the Hawks Nest Dam, leaving a pool of water with very little flow. Bottom; Aerial scene of the Drys. The river bed is exposed with pools of water since the main flow of the river is diverted through the tunnel.*

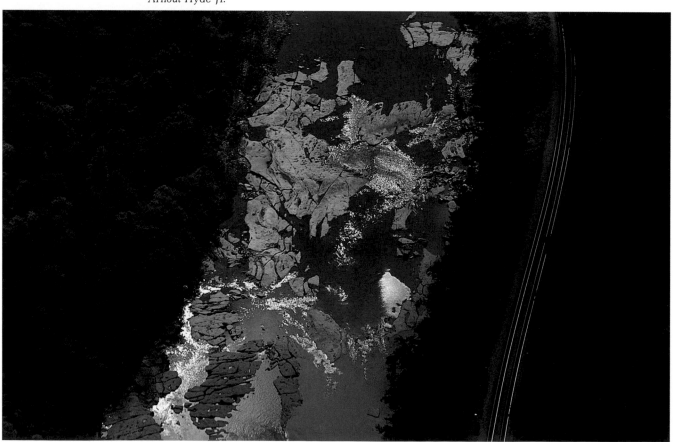

Arnout Hyde Jr.

Arnout Hyde J

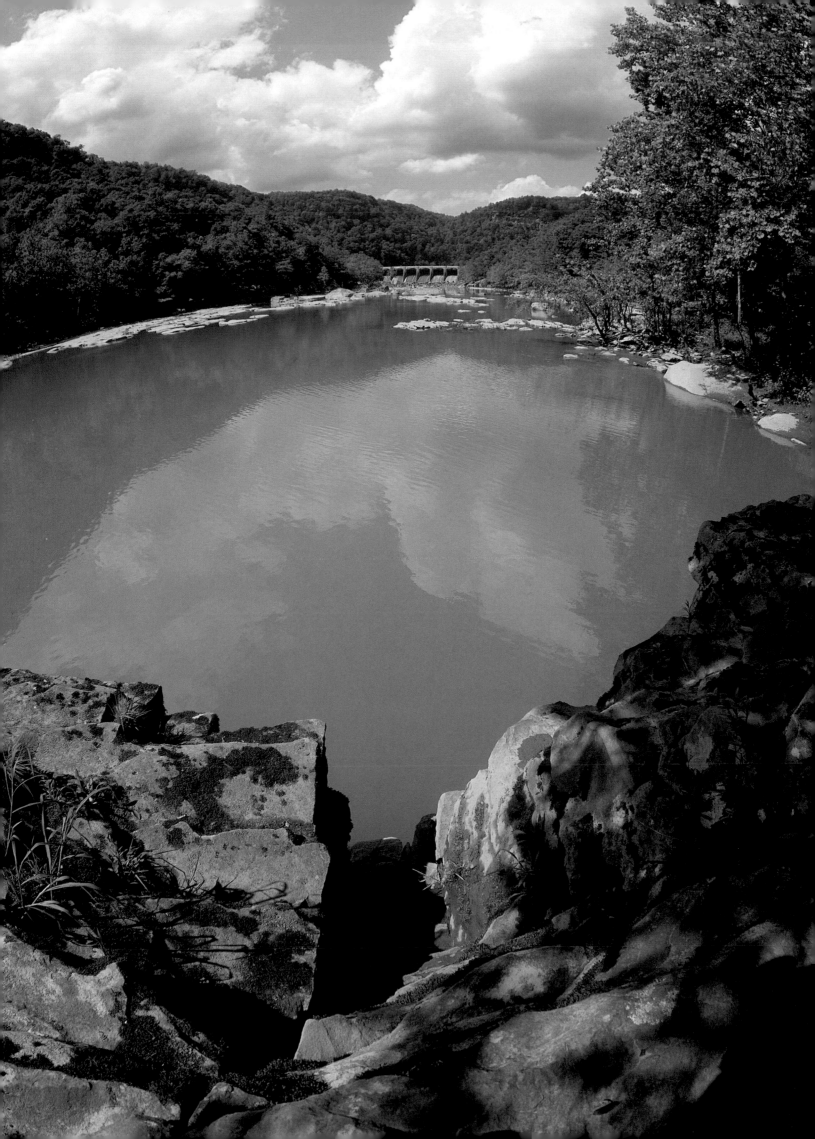

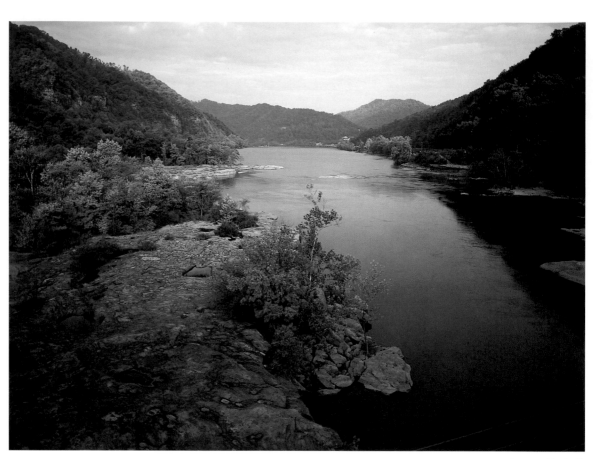

Looking down the New towards Gauley Bridge.

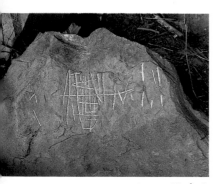

An unusual petroglyph at Beard's Fork several mountains away, which might be a possible ancient language

MYSTERIES IN THE GAULEY BRIDGE REGION

The confluence of the New and Gauley rivers, with the quaint town of Gauley Bridge, creates a beautiful setting between rugged mountains. Ancient stone walls, strange rock carvings, and a legend of a lost brass Civil War cannon are all tantalizing clues to past archaeological mysteries. Archaic stone walls, thousands of years old and several miles long, surround a nearby mountain. Archaeologists are baffled as to their purpose, since they were not high enough for defense fortifications. One theory is that they served some type of religious function. In the building of these stone walls, much of the stone was carried from the river below, a difficult task requiring large numbers of persons under a controlled society. Unfortunately, much of the wall was destroyed by strip mining.

A short distance from Gauley Bridge on Beards Fork, unusual petroglyphs (drawings) are carved on walls in a rock shelter. They resemble an ancient language with no likeness to the pictograph (pictorial symbol) which the American Indian was known to make. Some archaeologists and linguists think they are an ancient Irish language called Ogam, with a Christian message.

On the large flat rocks across the river from Gauley Mountain is a carved statue of a man holding a ship's wheel, which has been nicknamed "The Mariner." Origin of the artist and its meaning are unclear. Close by is a beautiful rock inscription with a Christian cross, an Italian name, the year 1893, and an overall resemblance to a coat of arms. The work appears to have been done by Italian stone masons, perhaps working on the railroad in the late 1800s.

There was activity during the Civil War around Gauley Bridge with fortifications still visible on the mountains overlooking the town. Stories of an abandoned brass cannon hidden in the hills close by still excite treasure hunters. Is it still there, covered with leaves and dirt?

Cultures that passed this way through the ages left fascinating glimpses into the past creating puzzling questions for modern man to ponder and study.

Right; *A beautiful rock carving, perhaps done by Italian stone masons in 1893. Below; A mysterious carving of a man resembling a mariner.*

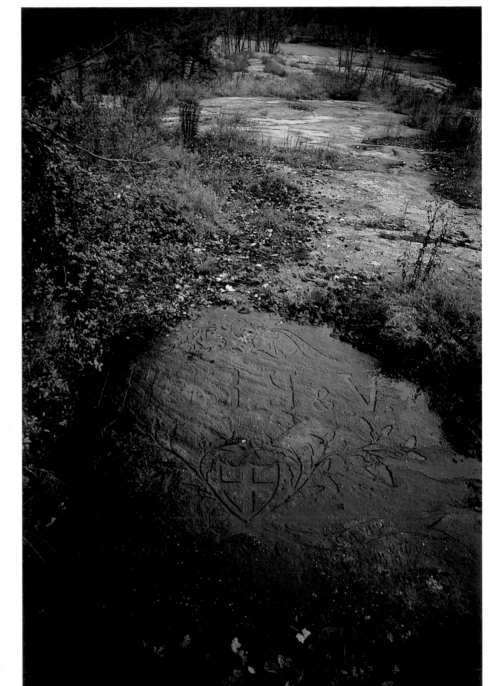

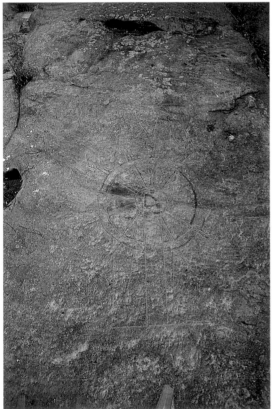

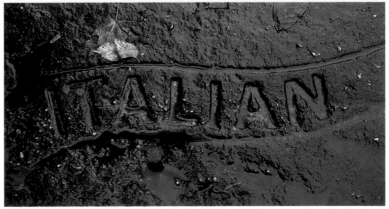

The word "Italian" seems to be raised; in actuality, it is indented into the rock, a photographic optical illusion.

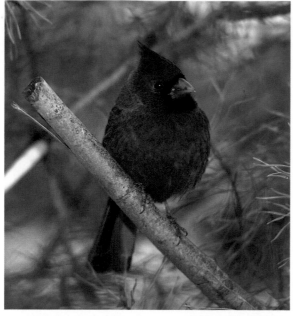

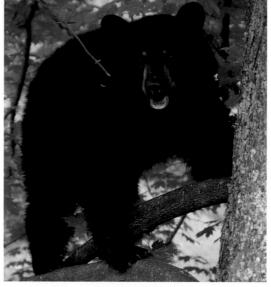

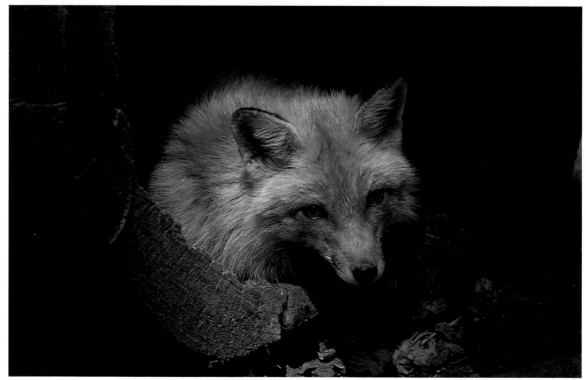

Above; Some of the wildlife seen along any section of the New River. These and many more species of wildlife that occur in the Appalachians can be observed along the banks of the river. Right; It would be difficult to do a book on the New River and not mention the Gauley River since they both share in being two of the finest whitewater rivers in the country. Also, both are under National Park Service jurisdiction. The Gauley is smaller than the New but is considered a more difficult whitewater river as the rapids are more numerous and complex. The same rafting companies that operate on the New also feature trips down this river, primarily in the fall when water is released from the Summersville Dam. Only the most experienced whitewater paddlers run the Gauley, and the rafting companies require rafters to first run the New for experience. More than one rafter has been heard to say, "Golly!" which pretty well describes this river.

A kayaker fights his way through Pillow Rock Rapid, one of the most exciting on the Gauley.

Overleaf; Morning sunrise over Gauley Bridge where the New River ends and joins the Gauley River, forming the Kanawha River.

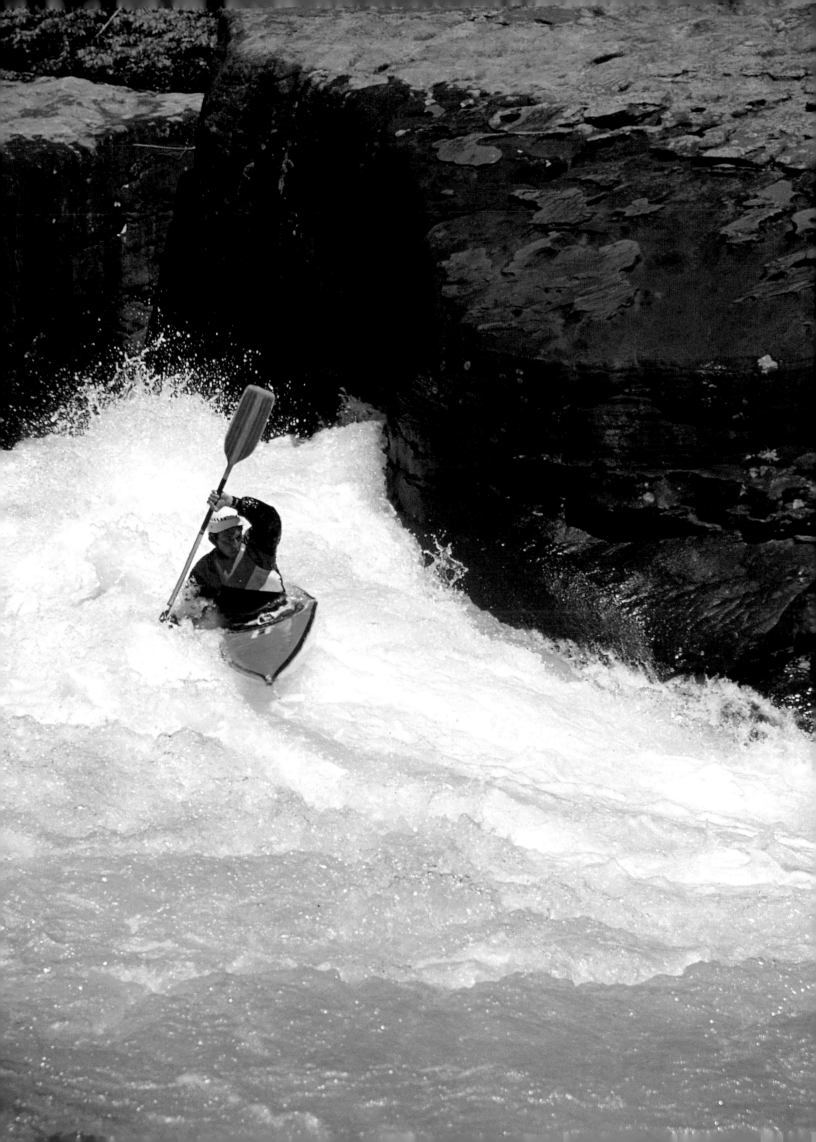